MW01252637

A LANGUAGE
FOR THE HEART

STEVEN MOSLEY

Pacific Press Publishing Association
Boise, Idaho
Oshawa, Ontario, Canada

Edited by Jerry D. Thomas
Designed by Tim Larson
Cover illustrations by Jim Converse and John Steel
Typeset in 10/12 Century Schoolbook

The author assumes full responsibility for the accuracy of all facts and quotations cited in this book.

Some material in this book adapted from:

Glimpses of God, *Finding the Father Who Fills Your Every Need*, Steven Mosley (Sisters, Oreg.: Questar Publishers, 1990).
 A Tale of Three Virtues, *Cures for Colorless Christianity,* Steven Mosley (Sisters, Oreg.: Questar Publishers, 1990).
 There I Go Again, *How to Keep From Falling for the Same Old Sin*, Steven Mosley (Irving, Tex.: Word Books, 1991).

Library of Congress Cataloging-in-Publication Data:

Mosley, Steven R., 1952-
   A language for the heart / Steven Mosley.
      p.   cm.
   ISBN 0-8163-1077-7
   1. Bible. O.T. Psalms—Criticism, interpretation, etc.
I. Title
BS1430.2.M59   1992
223' .206—dc20   91-33793
                                                        CIP

92 93 94 95 96 · 5 4 3 2 1

Contents

Chapter 1
It's OK to Ask Why

They have no struggles . . .
They are free from the burdens common to man.

The early sun cast long shadows as Asaph walked east through Jerusalem toward the Tent of Meeting. He'd told his wife he was going to polish the temple cymbals, but mostly he wanted to be alone this morning. Outwardly he stood as one of the most honored in his community, belonging to a prestigious Levitical clan. He and a colleague named Heman had been placed in charge of all temple music by royal decree; they often stood beside King David during great national ceremonies.

As Asaph walked by, the shepherds coming home from a night out in the fields, the carpenters and leather craftsmen working in their shops—all gave him a respectful greeting. Asaph returned a smiling "Shalom," but inside he was filled with anguished questions.

Why was it that Yahweh's most faithful followers were men and women who eked out an existence, barely making ends meet day after day? Why were the poor laborers the most pious? Or more important, why did the most pious remain poor laborers?

The sun rising over the Mount of Olives hit Asaph squarely in the face as he passed through the Gennath Gate, making him squint in the glare until the large house of Joseph the merchant cast out its formidable shadow.

It was a personal crisis that had started the temple musician's gloomy introspection. Problems in his family that no one looking on would have guessed. Problems at the temple with musicians who were misusing their position of trust. And his chronic illness.

Lately he'd woken up to each day as to some punishment, inflicted for unknown reasons by an inscrutable fate. And he hadn't been able to shake this sense of a plague hanging over him.

Just as Asaph trudged by the ornate, ivory-encrusted pillars of Joseph's portico, the merchant himself appeared on the roof, taking in the morning air. Two servant girls, perhaps concubines, were adjusting the beautiful purple robe he'd just put on. His gold and silver chains gleamed in the light.

Joseph looked down and caught Asaph's eye. Just then, Asaph bumped into two stray goats that were trotting through the narrow street. The merchant looked away, snorting in contempt, and took a wine glass from the hand of one of the girls. Asaph kicked at the slower of the goats and stomped off down the street. He couldn't get that face out of his mind. It was plump, oily, and cunning, yet without a care in the world.

How could such a man be blessed? Asaph wondered. This arrogant scoffer was so calloused that he'd sold a fellow Hebrew debtor into slavery, leaving the man's family destitute. Other merchants lived in fear of him; it was rumored he'd had one especially persistent rival killed.

And yet there he was, standing on the roof of the best house in Jerusalem, utterly free from the burdens common to all those simple folk who, unlike him, faithfully came to the temple each week. Everything that Asaph had ever been taught warred against this one terrible fact: Joseph was enjoying the good life.

Since childhood, Asaph had absorbed the teachings contained inside the ark that David had recently brought up to the Tent of Meeting. The covenant was enshrined there, the words of Moses, the eternal echo of Deuteronomy. Its litany of blessings and cursings had been drilled into him: the righteous are established, everything they put their hand to do prospers—crops, livestock, kneading trough, fruit of their womb—all blessed. The Lord opens His storehouse in heaven and pours out abundant prosperity on the obedient. But the wicked are cursed. Their crops and calves and lambs, the fruit of their womb—all cursed. They are struck with wasting disease, with blight and drought.

Asaph knew it all by heart. But that one malicious, fat face, the face of Joseph the merchant, seemed now more real than all those words of Scripture. And it gave the lie to all the principles he had based his life on. The more Joseph extorted and bullied his fellow men, the more prosperous he became. The more dishonest his practices, the more expensive spices, gold jewelry, and imported furniture he amassed.

Asaph had once overheard a scribe speaking with Joseph on one of his rare visits to the temple. The scribe had warned the merchant that Yahweh did not take kindly to the rich oppressing the poor. And Joseph had replied with perfect astonishment, "Does the Most High know everything?" It did not seem possible to the man that Yahweh concerned Himself with much that happened beyond the sacred precincts of the temple.

And that voice, filled with cynical skepticism, now loomed as large in Asaph's mind as the bloated face. It threatened to throw everything he believed into shadow. Did the Almighty indeed see everything? Had He overlooked the depredations of this evil man? Had He also overlooked the struggles of all the impoverished who called on His name?

And then a thought struck with a force more terrible than that of all the others he had entertained that morning: Maybe my lifelong effort to keep my heart pure before God has been for nothing. What if I have washed my hands in innocence all these years—and it really doesn't matter in the end?

Asaph stumbled against a wall and tried to steady himself. It seemed like a great weight threatened to crush him. In spite of the open air around the temple mount that clear morning, he seemed to be gasping for air in a thick, dank fog. Asaph shook his head violently, but his plummeting thoughts caught him again. Why do I put up with all my troubles at the temple? Just to lead the choir and plan a musical celebration? Why go on composing these psalms that the people mouth at Passover and Pentecost without understanding? What does it matter?

Asaph willed himself to walk through the temple courtyard toward the Tent of Meeting, and there planted his feet. He looked around, surrounded now by the symbols of Yahweh's world: the altar of burnt offering, the laver, and the white curtain stretching around him like a horizon. Asaph fell on his face there and shut his eyes. The questions were too much.

At some point, the temple musician came to himself and got up on his knees. The sun was visibly higher now, bearing down on the Tent of Meeting and making its purple and gold burn deep in the light. The cherubim woven in the curtains seemed almost animated. Asaph took it all in, and suddenly, everything became clear. He had an answer for that leering face above the best house in Jerusalem.

Why, O Lord?

The remarkable testimony that David's musician/poet Asaph has left us in Psalm 73 relates to a time in this man's life when he almost gave way to despair. The question Why? loomed over him as large and ominous as a beast from the Apocalypse. A God of righteous blessings clashed irreconcilably with the obvious injustices of the world. Why? This psalm is not so much an appeal for a tidy explanation as a cry from the heart, a cry for personal comfort. And it is not alone.

If the psalms are, by definition, vehicles of praise to the God of heaven, they often begin in a very unexalted state. The anguished question Why? finds an echo throughout the psalms.

Elsewhere in Scripture, we are assured that our heavenly Father will never leave us or forsake us. But the psalmists give voice to the unthinkable:

My God, my God, why have you forsaken me?

They even accuse the Almighty of being absent when needed most:

Why, O Lord, do you stand far off?
Why do you hide yourself in times of trouble?

The historical books of the Bible take pains to highlight Yahweh's spectacular triumphs through His servants—like that of Elijah on Mount Carmel. As the priests of Baal screamed to their god in vain, God's prophet taunted, "Shout louder! . . . Maybe he is sleeping and must be awakened." Then Elijah called down fire from heaven.

The psalmists, however, speak of those times when Elijah's cocksure question comes back to haunt us:

Awake, O Lord! Why do you sleep?
  Rouse yourself! Do not reject us forever.
Why do you hide your face
  and forget our misery and oppression?

Believers are often assured that our God is a Good Shepherd who tenderly cares for every member of His flock. He goes to great lengths to search out and rescue the one lost lamb. But sometimes we feel more abandoned than sheltered:

Why have you rejected us forever, O God?
  Why does your anger smolder against the sheep of
  your pasture?

We often affirm that God's right hand is strong to save. But there are dark days when another unspoken question haunts us:

Why do you hold back your hand, your right hand?

Every good churchgoer knows that God answers prayer, sometimes in spectacular ways. But there are times when He seems to turn a deaf ear to our pleas:

O Lord God Almighty,
  how long will your anger smolder
  against the prayers of your people?

We hear the prophets wax eloquent about how God cares for His people as faithfully and tenderly as a farmer cares for his prize vineyard—cultivating, watering, and pruning it with great solicitude. But the psalmists bore witness to occasions when God's own vineyard was spoiled. And they asked:

Why have you broken down its walls
  so that all who pass by pick its grapes?

Obviously the psalms are not just pretty pictures of God. They also give voice to our deepest feelings as human beings. We hear cries of desperation, of lostness, of perplexity, of sorrow, and even of terrible rage. These prayers to the Almighty come straight from the heart; they are not always dressed in their Sabbath best.

And so we sometimes hear things that are a bit shocking. Some psalms, for example, urge God to blot certain disreputable people out of the book of life or to dash the infants of the heathen against the rocks.

Scholars have gone to great lengths to explain these "imprecatory psalms" as stylized judicial statements quite different from your run-of-the-mill hateful diatribe. There is undoubtedly some truth to that, but I see a more important point made through those jagged shouts that creep up in the psalms. It is simply this: God listens.

I believe that's great news. It is perhaps the first thing we all need to know about God: He is willing to listen to us, no matter what we have to say. He doesn't open the portals of heaven only when we have composed a prayer fragrant with the appropriate pieties. He opens His ears and His heart when we are feeling depressed, when we can't think of one nice thing to say about so-and-so, when we aren't even sure He is really there or really cares, when we are mad enough to eat nails. God is a good listener.

The psalms are not always about God speaking; sometimes they are just about God listening. Of course, the overwhelming majority of the psalms do express sentiments that are directly inspiring. There are only six psalms that focus exclusively on getting even with personal enemies. Many more, of course, express personal devotion to God. Although several psalms express despair almost from beginning to end, about three times as many present desperate cries for help mixed with expressions of faith.

So it's pretty clear where God wants us to move: from a fix on our problems or enemies to a steady gaze at Him. But a few unedited, unsanctified prayers are there too. And they are there for a reason: to tell us that God listens to us from the very start. He hears our prayers before we can even pray in faith. He listens to our anger before we can focus it constructively.

God is a good listener. That's an important theme in the Psalms which is often overlooked. Those sometimes ragged, heated cries tell us that it's OK to ask why; it's OK to feel bad. God is listening.

I was a brute beast before you.
Yet I am always with you;
     you hold me by my right hand.

Asaph tells us in Psalm 73 that the lights went on for him when he "entered the sanctuary of God." I believe part of the reason he found a way out of his despair was his sudden realization that God had been listening all along. Even when he'd been ranting and raving senselessly, God had been taking it all in sympathetically and had begun to guide him to an answer.

Somewhere in that temple courtyard Asaph said to himself: "Wait a minute. Let's imagine that I never get much in the way of a material quality of life. What if I just manage to get by with enough food, clothing, and shelter—and that's it. I will still have known the God who is my portion forever. Isn't having a relationship with Him worth more in the balance than all the riches unscrupulous people can boast of?"

As the light dawned on him in the sanctuary, Asaph came to the point of affirming with some enthusiasm:

Whom have I in heaven but you?
     And being with you, I desire nothing on earth.

This man grew content as he contemplated what he now knew to be the bottom line in his life: "It is good to be near God." AMEN

That was one-half of the answer that Asaph stumbled into there at the Tent of Meeting. The other half concerned the ultimate fate of the wicked. He saw clearly that men like Joseph were really walking on slippery ground, ready at any moment to be swept away by terrors that no one on the outside can see. After it's all over and done, their lives will seem a dream.

There are, of course, other answers that we might want to give Asaph. We might want to talk about the great controversy and earth as the theater of the universe. We might even question whether Asaph's answer is fully Christian. Are we supposed to take comfort in the downfall of the immoral?

But the point is that Asaph received an answer to Why? that satisfied him on an emotional level. He found an insight that stilled his very personal cry of anguish.

And often that's what we need too. Sometimes all those head answers, the logical reasons why, don't do us much good. When the guy down the street gets lung cancer, answers on an intellectual level are usually enough. We can understand why evil has broken out on this planet and is running its course. But when our spouse gets leukemia, we need an answer on an emotional level. The overall plan for the universe isn't enough. Talk about big Whys echoes hollow. We want God to tell us about this particular Why. We want an answer that reaches our broken hearts.

The psalms tell us that the Almighty does indeed give us such answers. We do find Him down there in the darkest pits; we do hear a voice that breaks open the horizon-to-horizon gloom. Many of the psalms are testimonies to that effect.

But here's the catch. To receive answers on an emotional level, you have to become a good listener. Soul-satisfying insights aren't notes from heaven we may pick up casually at a post-office box. We have to listen carefully for them.

Thank God that He first models this important behavior for us. He listens intently as we pour out our hearts—as if we were the only ones in the universe speaking to Him. God can give us that kind of attention. And He inspires a similar receptivity in return. We need to give God our full attention in prayer; we need to listen carefully if we are to hear a language for the heart.

This does not mean that we have to become mystics and try to hear voices or see visions. It simply means that we give God quality time in prayer and Bible study. We just have to listen.

When overwhelmed with despair, Asaph was tempted to go in two directions, both away from listening. First he tells us that his feet almost slipped; he nearly lost his foothold. That is, this man almost did decide to quit keeping his heart pure "in vain." If things are a mess, why not sin a little?

That's a natural response to perplexity. We loosen up our moral lifestyle in direct proportion to how unsure we become about God's truth being in place. We don't want to make any great sacrifices if heaven is less of a sure thing. This is usually not a conscious choice but something we drift into.

However, slipping into sin and listening to God create dissonance;

the two don't go together. Something has to give. So usually, if we are indulging in shady activities, we try to keep God's voice at arm's length. We give the Scriptures á cursory glance; we toss the Lord a quick greeting in the morning or avoid these practices altogether.

But Asaph was not willing to do that. He had to keep hearing his Lord, up close and personal. He would not react to perplexity by sinning—getting back at God by wandering away from Him.

To keep times of anguish from pushing us into transgression, we must commit ourselves to keep talking and keep listening. If we are ever to find an answer that satisfies our heart, it will be in God's still small voice, not through some quick, little sin.

The other pitfall that Asaph avoided in his time of trial was bitterness. When that attitude began to sink in—"my heart was grieved and my spirit embittered"—he didn't mope about the house and nourish those feelings; he went to the temple.

Every loss we experience in life requires a certain amount of mourning. Sadness is a normal, healthy response to the bad things that happen to us. Sadness turns to bitterness only when we rehearse the loss over and over to ourselves—and find no outlet for the sorrow. Asaph dealt with the problem of bitterness by opening up to God. He kept talking and kept listening, even though much of what he said in the beginning was only ugliness. But his pouring out these feelings to the Father prevented them from hardening into a mind-set: life is the pits, and God doesn't care.

We become bitter when we stop listening to God. Rummaging around and around in our own pain is a dead end. We need to find a way out—not by ignoring the pain but by laying it before God and attempting to be what He is: a good listener. No matter how unpromising the feelings we bring to the Father, if we give Him time, He will speak to us in a language that satisfies the heart.

Chapter 2
Pouring It All Out

Heart cry

Everyone always thought of Kazko as the perfect child. Relatives and neighbors dropping by the Nozaki household never heard her complain or whine or beg for things. She was always so helpful to her mother. She seemed mature beyond her years and took on responsibilities well. Kazko's aunts would often pat her on the head and say what a brave little girl she was, growing up without a father and never being a burden on her mother.

Kazko's dad had died shortly after World War II, when she was only two. Mr. Nozaki was a wonderful man whom she would come to admire many years later from stories his devoted business associates told. After becoming aware that he had contracted a terminal illness, he worked very hard at his company and managed to leave his family a sizable sum. But after his death, an uncle, whose alcohol problem and poor business sense mixed ominously, had talked Kazko's mother into investing the savings in a venture that proved disastrous.

So Mrs. Nozaki had to try to earn a living on her own—no easy task in postwar Japan. She became a teacher of koto, the traditional stringed instrument that young women of good breeding were expected to study. For much of the year, Mrs. Nozaki had to teach in the southern island of Kyushu. Kazko and her sister stayed with their grandmother.

Through all this Kazko tried very hard to act the part of the perfect child. She was very aware of what a struggle it was for her mother to try to support two little girls alone. She tried very hard not to be a burden.

14

Kazko learned not to ask for things—she must remain the brave little girl in these difficult circumstances. And her mother remained distant during these years—emotionally as well as physically. This woman was still handicapped by her own childhood deprivations. Her mother had given her away to an aunt when she was four years old. The wounds that resulted from this break in the bonding process were being repeated, generation after generation.

Fast forward a few decades to southern California. Kazko is now my wife and the happy mother of our two children. Like most kids, they occasionally whine and beg for things they want. And like most parents, we try to keep this to a minimum. But Kazko hears in their plaintive voices something I do not. It's the sound of a child who can ask a parent for anything, the sound of a child secure enough to plead. This is a language she could never learn in her formative years. She could never come freely and comfortably to Dad or Mom and just pour out the desires of her heart.

So even though, as a mother, Kazko must carefully decide what the kids can and cannot get by begging, there is comfort as well as discomfort for her in the sometimes-shrill sound of their pleas. She is listening to the echo of an innocent, spontaneous language that she, in a different time and different place, might once have spoken.

Answer me, for I am poor and needy

There is a distinct language that we may trace throughout the psalms of Scripture, a tone and a cadence that suggest a child coming before a parent and pouring it all out. The psalms cry out for help. Forty-one of them are dominated by pleas for rescue. The verses tumble out directly and simply—help me; I'm in trouble. We see people appealing to God, often desperately, in all kinds of situations.

David's perils dominate early on. Psalms 52-60 picture him pleading for help on the run—hiding from Saul, fleeing from the Philistines, always in fear of betrayal or ambush.

In Psalm 38, we find David enduring some traumatic illness: his wounds fester and are loathsome; his back is filled with searing pain; there is no health in his body; even the light has gone from his eyes. The author of Psalm 71 makes us painfully aware of another kind of physical affliction: the atrophy of old age.

Psalm 137 is the bitter cry of exiles whose captors demand that they sing songs of a lost Jerusalem. In Psalm 74, an anguished cry for help rises out of the ruins of the holy sanctuary, smashed and broken with axes, burned to the ground.

The psalms often break into urgent language. The verses bunch into short bursts, evoking the rhythm of a person rocking back and forth in grief. These appeals spring up because ruthless enemies threaten or moral decay lies in wait, because national calamity looms or personal crisis erupts.

If you read through the psalms, all these cries for help may put you off at first glance. They can start to sound like so much whining. And anyway, it's not often that we are hounded by these vicious enemies who so heavily populate the book.

But it's important to remember that these psalms reflect centuries of Israel's history. They highlight momentous occasions in the lives of the Hebrew people. Human beings are most often moved to compose great prayers in times of crisis. Ask yourself when you have been most eloquent before the Father. Isn't it usually when you are about to go off some cliff and are pleading for all you're worth? That's when we come to God most earnestly. What's remarkable is the number of times that the psalmists' cries for help, even in the worst of circumstances, turn into sounds of praise.

But there's another reason for the forty-one urgent appeals recorded in the psalms; it's a very basic lesson that sometimes slips by us. God is simply telling us: "It's OK to ask." We can come to Him as freely as a child running to a parent. We may not always ask for the right things; God will certainly not always answer us in the way we prescribe. But He does invite us to come. We have the privilege of using the innocent, spontaneous language of children who are secure in their parents' unconditional acceptance.

Some believers have grown up in the faith in a manner not unlike the way my wife Kazko grew up. They are always trying to live up to the high expectations of the religious "relatives" around them. They try so hard to look good before these external standards. And they try never to be a burden on God; they never come pleading for things like other "immature" children of the Father. They try to stand up straight (on their own) and follow the divine example (at a distance).

Becoming more like our Father is certainly a big part of Christian life. The language of obedience is important to learn. But that process will harden into legalism unless we also learn another language: "Please." "I need."

Before we are anything else, we are needy children, totally dependent on our parents. That is true at the beginning of physical life, at the beginning of spiritual life, and at the start of every day of our Christian life. It's good to know the language of "help." The psalms show us that it's good to be secure enough to come and plead at the feet of the Father who cherishes us.

An old story tells of a rabbit frantically skittering around bushes as it attempts to escape from a dog in hot pursuit. Sympathetic bystanders shout approval: "You're doing great. Run a bit harder, and you'll get away."

"Thanks for your kind encouragement," the rabbit replies, "but for pity's sake, shoot the dog!"

Although it's fine for us to take encouragement from the fact we can cry out to God for help, we still have to wonder: Does anything happen as a result? Does anybody shoot the dog? If the psalmists often make their appeals while running from ruthless enemies, does the God they cry to deal with those enemies?

The reassuring testimony of many psalms is that He does. God doesn't just listen, He acts.

David's desperation, for example, often ends in enthusiastic testimony. He can proclaim: "You lifted me out of the depths" and "brought me up from the grave" in Psalm 30. On another occasion, when he'd escaped once again from the clutches of obsessive King Saul, David exclaimed:

> He reached down from on high and took hold of me:
>   he drew me out of deep waters.

Yahweh, it is affirmed, does more than answer with comforting words:

> You answer us with awesome deeds of righteousness,
>   O God our Saviour.

Even after passing through difficult ordeals, the psalmists often see God's hand at work:

> You let men ride over our heads;
>   we went through fire and water,
>   but you brought us to a place of abundance.

Sometimes God's response is to do something inside the petitioner:

> When I called, you answered me;
>   you made me bold and stouthearted.

Sometimes He delivers dramatically:

> In my anguish I cried to the Lord,
>   and he answered by setting me free.
> The Lord is with me; I will not be afraid.
>   What can man do to me?

The psalms often juxtapose desperation and deliverance. We move from the unthinkable horror of the temple ravaged in Psalm 74 to the exultant shouts of Psalm 76, reflecting, according to ancient tradition, the Lord's miraculous destruction of Sennacherib's besieging army.

In the psalms, God acts; He comes through. We come running to Him as trusting children, not just because He is empathetic but also because He is Almighty; Daddy can do anything. The psalmists, in fact, liked to dramatize this divine response to human plea in terms of elemental forces unleashed.

Psalm 18, for example, pictures God parting the heavens and riding down on the cherubim as the earth quakes. Hailstones and lightning are propelled out of the brightness of His presence. He causes His enemies to scatter like men fleeing from a shower of arrows. He rescues those who delight in Him.

This is a victorious Warrior who contends with all who dare to contend with the children He cherishes. These images of God rending the heavens and shaking the earth echo the language of children comparing their respective fathers: "My dad is so strong he could . . ." They celebrate God's omnipotence: He can do anything. We can have the confidence that, not only does God listen, but He also acts on our behalf.

One summer night, a Scottish youth decided to take a shortcut across the moors on his way to Bamburgh, where he had a job. This Northumberland countryside was noted for its limestone, and one deep, deserted quarry lay nearby along Glororum Road. But the lad thought he could avoid it.

Even though the night was starless, inky black, he set out through the rock and heather. He could sometimes hear the far-off bleating of sheep, and the wind rustling; occasionally a moor fowl he disturbed fluttered up noisily. Otherwise he was very much alone in the night.

Suddenly he heard a voice call out with great urgency, "Peter!"

The youth, a bit unnerved, stopped and called back into the dark, "Yes, who is it? What do you want?"

No response. Just a bit of wind over the deserted moorland.

The lad concluded he'd been mistaken and walked on a few more steps. But then he heard the voice again, more urgent than before: "Peter!"

He stopped in his tracks, bent forward to peer through the dense black, and stumbled to his knees. Reaching out a hand to the ground before him, he clutched thin air. The quarry! Sure enough, as Peter carefully felt around in a semicircle, he discovered he had stopped on the edge of the abandoned limestone quarry—one step before a fatal plunge into the deep.

Out there in the desolate moor, Peter Marshall encountered the victorious Warrior who rescues. It certainly seemed to him that God had parted the heavens and rushed down on the wings of the wind for his personal benefit. This young man dedicated his life to the One who'd plucked him from the pit—calling him by name—and became one of America's most respected ministers.

Your right hand

The psalmists assure us that we can take any and every problem to the God who is strong to save. But they also tell us how that process should end.

Whining can be a problem. It is possible to go on and on, moaning about how terrible things are. Our kids are a mess; our job is the pits; our church is full of lukewarm believers. We can turn our freedom with God into a long complaint session.

Our Father does want us to bring all our concerns before Him, but He doesn't want us to become problem centered. How do we keep pouring out our hearts before God and yet avoid staring at spilled milk all the time?

The psalms themselves give us a clue. Out of the forty-one psalms in which cries for help are the major theme, thirty-one end in an anthem of praise. That is, the majority manage to move from anguish to expectation, from a focus on the problem to the solution.

And what is the solution? God the victorious Warrior. He is the bright image on whom our gaze must rest in the end, after we've unburdened ourselves of our fears and frustrations. He has to be the last picture we look at. His right hand, strong to save, is more important than our feeble fumbling.

There is another reason Yahweh is pictured in these dramatic terms as the God who flashes around in the cosmos. His dynamic movement creates spiritual momentum for us.

Just as God the good Listener both inspires and enables us to become careful listeners ourselves, so the God of action inspires us to join Him in action.

The pleas in our prayers need to find a healthy climax in a plan of action. Prayer is most answerable when it seizes on divine initiatives, reaching out to meet needs with divine resources. This, more than anything else, distinguishes those whose prayers seem to trigger acts of providence from those whose prayers seem to trickle away without a trace. The former tend to be active, seeking to carry out God's purposes by His means. The latter tend to be passive, reacting to things that threaten their comfort or security.

Why do all those great stories of miraculous answers to prayer seem to come from African jungle villages or obscure Chinese provinces? Why does it appear that God is visibly active only in the mission field? A skeptic might assume that providential drama gets added in the translation as the stories are passed along from hinterland to American Sabbath School. A bigger reason, I think, is that God is most active when we are reaching out most. He stretches out when we stretch out.

God is active in the thick of it. George Whitefield met his fiercest opposition and most dramatic conversions while preaching in the open air at a London fairgrounds full of strolling players, bear baiters, merry-andrews, pickpockets, and gin sellers. When Whitefield drew large crowds around his makeshift platform, he aroused the ire of more secular showmen. They tried mocking him and then shouting him down—both without success. Then they picked up a huge maypole and charged the outer edge of the crowd. This battering ram was dangerous. If any were struck by the pole, bones could break, and even worse, men and women could die in the crush to get away.

Whitefield paused in his sermon, shouted a warning to the crowd, and began to pray aloud, asking the Lord of hosts to hearken and intervene. Suddenly the group of rowdies running with their cumbersome projectile began yelling and gesturing at each other. A dispute erupted. They dropped the maypole and began flailing away at each other. Finally the leaders slunk off. Some of the men, however, decided to stay, and a few were actually converted.

We will never experience the joy of great answers to prayer as long as we spend most of our time on the couch, sending out occasional petitions like remote-control signals and waiting for some act of providence to show up like an entertaining TV show. Miracles are a participant phenomenon; they rarely happen to bystanders. If we're waiting for God to perform for us as we relax in the pew or living room, we'll witness very little.

The psalmists picture a dramatically active God in order to sweep us up in His activity. Obscure Chinese provinces and African villages don't have a lock on God's miraculous intervention. He is active wherever people are reaching out.

I'll never forget the first time I caught a sense that God and I had made a rendezvous, that we were acting together to make things happen. I was in college. Mark and I were heading into the student union at Western Illinois University for our weekly round of cold-turkey witnessing. On this day, we had a rather tenuous hold on our zeal and our *Four Spiritual Laws* booklets. In the eatery jammed with the sounds of "A Horse With No Name" and the chattering of undergraduates, we wondered if anyone would really listen. Weary of running up against wall-to-wall disinterest, we decided to pray together for open people, students who would respond. We wanted to see the Word bear fruit for a change.

The first two guys we talked with were friendly skeptics. One, it turned out, was a former Adventist, so I could talk about his disillusionment with the church and how a relationship with Jesus had made all the difference for me. The next guy we ran into was an acquaintance of Mark's who planned to become a priest. Then we met a student who had been "wondering about things" because of his Christian Scientist roommate. He appeared to be earnestly searching. We had a good talk and planned to meet again. The last guy we spoke with prayed to receive Christ as his Saviour.

As Mark and I walked out of the student union, we were electric with the *zap* of making contact. Our wandering around the crowded tables didn't seem random at all now. It was as if God and the two of us had met at some secretly prearranged point and made a discernible impact.

Chapter 3

Memory: Lost and Found

They remembered the Rock

Every time Mr. Thompson was brought to see his neurologist, Dr. Oliver Sacks, he would mistake the doctor for a variety of other characters—all people from his past, one after the other. After being seated in the office, this man would usually start by asking Dr. Sacks if he wanted any special cheese today, thinking him a customer at his old delicatessen. Then he'd correct himself and greet "Tom Pitkins," an old friend who used to accompany him to the races. Next he would see the physician's white coat and realize with a start, "You're Hymie, the kosher butcher next door. No bloodstains on your coat, though. Business bad today?" Then he'd spot the stethoscope and exclaim, "You mechanics are all starting to fancy yourselves to be doctors . . . so, you're my old friend Manners from the Mobil station."

Mr. Thompson went through this ritual, not because his eyesight was failing or his intelligence gone, but because of a peculiar loss of memory. He was suffering from a severe form of amnesia known as Korsakoff's psychosis. He couldn't remember anything for longer than several seconds. It wasn't just that a section of his past life had dropped out of conscious recollection but that everything that happened to him, everything he thought, was continually being lost—irrecoverably. This left him perpetually disoriented. Anyone who spoke to him and then left the room for the briefest moment would come back a complete stranger to Mr. Thompson.

In working with this patient, Dr. Sacks was struck by the tragedy of a man who "must literally make himself (and his world) up every moment . . . throwing bridges of meaning over abysses of meaninglessness."

As a result, Mr. Thompson babbled on continually, spinning tales about his past. To the people who knew him, he seemed like "a man in a race, a man trying to catch something which always eludes him." What he could never grasp was any real sense of self, what Dr. Sacks described as "a life-story, an inner narrative— whose continuity, whose sense, is our lives."

Another story that documents the tragedy brought about by a loss of memory is found in Psalm 78. It's the story of Israel, a people whose epic began gloriously in a miraculous passage through the Red Sea. They proceeded on through wilderness adventures overseen by Yahweh, the desert Sentinel, in a cloud by day and fiery pillar by night. These former slaves drank water that flowed from rocks, ate manna that fell from heaven, and feasted on quail carried to their feet by a strong wind. Finally, their God drove out the occupants of Canaan before them and settled them in a land flowing with milk and honey.

But through this dramatic history, the Hebrews couldn't shake a persistent problem: the loss of memory. "They did not remember his power" exhibited through all the miraculous signs that had safeguarded their exit from Egypt. Out of sight, out of mind. As soon as the haze cleared from some display of divine power, and the children of Israel found themselves trudging in the wilderness, bereft of leeks and onions, they defaulted into the "What have you done for us lately?" mode. A failure of memory led to a process of complaint, anger, rebellion, and apostasy.

By contrast, the good times of national revival and restoration could usually be traced to a recovery of memory: "They remembered that God was their Rock."

Psalm 78 itself is an attempt to re-create memory for a people plagued by this recurring amnesia. The psalmist begins his poem by pledging to pass on to the next generation "things our fathers have told us." He hopes that children yet unborn will share the story with their descendants.

> Then they would put their trust in God
>   and would not forget his deeds

but would keep his commands.

Without a strong memory, people have to make themselves up as they go along. And this naturally follows whatever impulses dominate at the moment. Life gets pretty erratic. Israel lost its distinctive and redemptive identity as a people by forgetting the divine highlights of their past. We can lose our identity in the same way. And the end result is to get lost, like Mr. Thompson, in a web of tales and an endless race that barely keeps us going from one moment to the next.

If I forget you, O Jerusalem

The generic PC that I use in my writing has one maddening peculiarity. It freezes up when I add more than a certain amount of information to any one file. I wish I knew exactly what amount that is. I can usually get 6,000 words into a file, but sometimes, when my computer is feeling particularly lethargic, it refuses to digest even less. Sometimes, I have gone on keying in paragraph after paragraph, feeling like I'm really on a roll. Then I remember to save the information to the computer's memory. I press the keys to initiate that function—and the screen freezes up. I can't move the cursor; no signals get through. The only thing I can do is turn off the computer and start again.

But this means I have lost everything I wrote that wasn't saved, wasn't recorded, in the computer. All those words just went down the drain.

My PC also gets cranky when I have to perform several complex functions in succession, like moving or rearranging documents. Then it can freeze up without warning no matter how little I have in a file. A few days ago my computer bowed out twice on me in one morning, so I ended up having to write part of a certain chapter in this book three times. Needless to say, I got rather irritated. As I tried to re-create what I had written—for the third time—I found myself pounding on the keys, indignantly banging out the words (that were supposed to form nice sentences on edifying religious themes).

What I really wanted to do was put my foot through the monitor, but I didn't want to buy a new one. I settled on yelling and pounding on my long-suffering desk instead (in between nice, spiritual paragraphs).

Recently, I had a neighbor who's something of a computer whiz come over and check out my recalcitrant machine. He informed me that everything seemed OK except for a glitch in the memory. That was the problem. Somewhere in that tiny labyrinth a circuit was saying No instead of Yes. A path was blocked—and that made everything freeze up.

Since then I have realized that my blankety-blank computer and I have something in common: our memory seems to go when the pressure heats up. Most mornings when I sit down at my desk and look out the window, I feel extremely grateful that I can do what I love, that is, write, and make a living at it. And what's more, I can write about the things I care about most deeply—and still earn a living. I usually tell God about this, thanking Him for the privilege.

But when I stare at a frozen screen and realize that every sentence I have labored to put down just right has disappeared into thin air—I forget all about that privilege. I see only this inscrutable computer that has turned on me again, and I slip into a you've-ruined-my-whole-day routine.

Actually, the material lost, compared to the whole of the script or book I'm working on, is usually quite small. And I can rewrite it in a few minutes. But if I'm in a bad mood, that perspective doesn't break through. The molehill instantly turns to a mountain, and I find myself flailing away at it.

Anger gets out of hand and our day is ruined most often because of a lack of perspective. Think about it. Is the clod who happened to swerve in front of you on the freeway really out to destroy you and your entire family? Is the cancellation of that dinner engagement really the end of life as we know it on this planet?

Perspective helps us zoom those mountains down to molehills again; we have a horizon to compare things with. But perspective requires a good memory. That's the key. We have to have the bigger picture there in our minds if we are to fit smaller irritants into it.

We have to remember what a privilege it is to work for and with Christ. We have to remember what of importance has stayed the same when some cog in the system gets out of whack.

In these psalms that telescope the history of Israel, we can see an attempt to give people perspective, memory. The composer of Psalm 136 turns history into one refrain repeated from beginning to end: "His love endures forever." That's the point of all the events he lists; that's the cue that should trigger these good memories when times get hard.

Psalms 40 and 44 are acts of remembering in the tough times, when the authors had been brought down to the dust. In desperation, the psalmists turned to memory—and found that:

> Many, O Lord my God,
>   are the wonders you have done.

The writer of Psalm 143 penned these words beside his cries for an answer:

> I remember the days of long ago;
>   I meditate on all your works
>   and consider what your hands have done.
> I spread out my hands to you;
>   my soul thirsts for you like a parched land.

It's easy to remember when the birds are cheery and the sky radiant. What counts is remembering when the storm clouds gather. Faith is simply the willingness to say, "Yes, things don't look very bright right now, but I remember and affirm how God came through in the past."

The psalmists didn't forget in the bad times because they knew God never forgets. Even when His chosen people wandered into idolatry again and again, "he remembered that they were but flesh."

Telling of all your wonderful deeds

One good way to strengthen our own memory is to keep a journal that chronicles the acts of God in our lives. The book of Psalms in particular, and the Bible in general, is an exercise in documenting His gracious activity. Many of the psalms appear almost like diary entries, personal accounts of some event and what the author experienced about God as a result. The writers of Scripture often urge us to do the same. Psalm 77 is a testimony of how memory saved the writer from despair. He vows: "I will meditate on all your works and consider all your mighty deeds." Another psalmist tells us to "remember the wonders he has done."

Most of Israel's festivals were designed to remind them of Jehovah's saving acts on their behalf. The Hebrews were encouraged to regularly repeat the stories of God's deliverance.

We need a way to remember and treasure God's acts on our behalf. Many answers to prayer encourage us greatly at the time but afterward fade into the vague past. The vivid outline of God's hand that once thrilled us grows hazy in the distance. Forgotten blessings lose their power to strengthen our faith.

It's good to hear about God's miracles in history but even more edifying are the acts He performs for us individually. When I began focusing my journal on God's actions, my perspective changed. He became more than the Saviour of the world; He was my Lord. We were in a joint venture. As I review the specific instances of His graciousness, that accumulation of evidence moves me to a livelier faith.

One incident I take pleasure in remembering happened while I was teaching English in Japan.

This morning something hit me hard. I want to be useful. Now. There are so many needs around and I just pass people by, oblivious. Jesus promised that the works He did we will do. So I prayed that God would lead me today to someone I can help.

After my 10:30 class, Clair stopped me in the hall and asked if she could talk with me after staff meeting. Just like that, out of the blue. In the afternoon we went into the Bible room. She began spilling out how totally inadequate she felt as a student missionary: "How can I tell others about Jesus? I don't know Him at all."

We talked for quite a while about how she could re-establish her devotional life; we got into the nitty-gritty. It was good—and so great to see God respond, just like that, out of the blue.

God ceases to be abstract when we see Him at work. Records of our encounters with His grace help fill out His character. He becomes more than a black-and-white moral outline. In action, He appears in living color. And that is what sticks in our memory.

At first, we might wonder if we will ever have any miracles to report. Most of us don't see the Red Sea parted every week or experience narrow escapes from a lions' den. We do more regularly, however, see evidences of a God who cares, of One who cooperates with us when we seek His help. Writing about these incidents sharpens our eye. We become more aware of God's guidance and protection in the jumble of daily events.

One of the most profitable ways we can use a personal journal is as a companion to Bible study. Most of us have had precious moments with the Scriptures when some promise or principle impressed us deeply. Maybe we see a familiar verse as if for the first time, and for a while its meaning shines clear. But in time the intensity of our insight tends to weaken. Other things crowd out the memory.

However, by keeping a record of what God teaches us through Scripture, we can relive those refreshing times of revelation. Once, while feeling quite discouraged about my same old struggle with the same old sins, I read about how the priest Jehoiada orchestrated a brilliant coup. That narrative (see 2 Kings 11) inspired me to fight more effectively.

Yes, it would be great to overcome as if in Jehoiada's palace plot: muster up all the priests in Jerusalem, surround the court with armed guards, seat Joash on the throne, and lead a great crowd in acclaiming him king. When unscrupulous Queen Athaliah rushes out to check on the noise, she is forced to throw in the towel.

Don't just trudge out with your small shield and try to fend off the flesh, the world, and the devil. Go out with a massive show of force. Stuff yourself with the Word until you are surrounded by God's promises, wonders, commands, and righteousness. Get on the offensive, with praise. Overwhelm the devil; don't duel with him.

The very act of writing down an idea tends to reinforce what we've learned. Putting our insight into words focuses our thinking and crystallizes God's point. Also, the fact that we plan to record something often stimulates us to make more discoveries. Instead of just settling for a vaguely uplifting time in the Word, we dig up truths of practical value.

In time, a journal can become the commentary of our lives on the precision of Scripture. As we gain experience in applying its principles and claiming its promises, the Word becomes flesh in a new, individual way. We see it come through for us.

Personal journals are also a way to stop and think. They help us reflect for a while about where we've been and where we're going. There are few things more tragic than an unexamined life.

We build a healthy memory not just by recording events but also by our reactions to them—what we feel and think. A little reflection will often help clarify our values and thus soften some of life's blows. It can teach us the relative importance of a new sedan as compared to the laughter of our children or remind us of how much we used to treasure moments of communication with our spouse.

Sometimes we discover great value in something easily overlooked. Take a dull church sprinkled with a few silver-haired ladies . . .

> The service had finally trickled to a close. I slouched lazily in a rear pew as the smattering of worshipers filed out. Several women seated by the aisle remained, bowing in the quiet. One elderly gentleman, seated by himself toward the front of the church, slowly rose from his pew. He fumbled for a huge book, thickened by Braille lettering, and slipped it under his arm.
>
> As the man began to make his way uncertainly toward the rear, one of the grandmothers reached out and clasped his hands tightly. They exchanged a few animated words. Then the next woman at the aisle held the gentleman's hand, and the next, each one beaming up to him a greeting. In this way they formed an unobtrusive escort, guiding his steps toward the rear of the building, giving him their human warmth as fellow pilgrims.
>
> I looked up, and the man's face transfixed me. Around sunken, glazed eyes, his features radiated an intense joy. The women's hands had broken through his isolation and he exulted in the moment.

God wants us to fashion the language of memory out of life itself. Sometimes His meanings lie just below the surface; our everyday surroundings are sometimes bursting with His signs. It is our privilege to meet God's messages in unexpected places.

After suction failed, our doctor grabbed these nasty-looking forceps. Big claws they were. I cringed as he got a hold on our infant and pulled hard. But all of a sudden, swish, the baby was there, plopped down soft and warm on Kaz's belly. I tried to keep my camera and eyes going at the same time, not wanting to miss anything live. Nonchalantly, nervously, I check nose, mouth, fingers, feet—all there. A perfect firstborn son.

Then it struck me. Could Christ have been like this? God Almighty smudged with dark blood, squinting in the strangeness, head distended, limbs unwieldy as crowbars. For the first time, I saw the Incarnation.

His Father had to stand and wait too, taking a back seat to donkeys and shepherds. The One whose hands had not lost their skill since fashioning the orchids and gazelles of this planet had to be hidden, disarmed. It was a potent love welling up in Jehovah that opened His hands and delivered the Infant into our calloused ones.

All of us have moments when God's grace comes near. A journal is a way of looking more closely and turning moments into good memory, that "inner narrative—whose continuity, whose sense, is our lives." In creative remembering we can stretch our thoughts toward true wisdom, multiply our thanksgiving, fire our faith, incite heartfelt praise, and build a divine sensitivity to all of life.

Chapter 4
When Darkness Is Your Only Friend

Watchmen, wait for the morning

A young man who attempted unsuccessfully to kill himself with a pistol related to psychologist Edwin Schneidman what might be called a postsuicide note. This is how he described his experience:

> I had done all I could and I was still sinking. I sat many hours seeking answers, and all there was was a silent wind.
>
> Then a friend offered to sell me a gun. I bought it. That day I began saying goodbye to people . . . silently. My mind became locked on my target. My thought was: Soon it will all be over. I would obtain the peace I had so long sought. The will to survive and succeed had been crushed and defeated. . . . I felt I had to have the upper hand, to control my environment, so I sought to die rather than surrender. . . .
>
> I was only aware of myself and my plight. Death swallowed me long before I pulled the trigger. The world through my eyes seemed to die with me. . . . There comes a time when all things cease to shine, when the rays of hope are lost.

Words like these are part of the blunt, despairing language that Dr. Schneidman has been analyzing for forty years. He's compiled detailed mental histories, called psychological autopsies, which have shed light on why people try to commit suicide.

This young man simply saw no hope, no other way out but death. He'd done all he could, he thought, but was still sinking. One characteristic of the suicidal is a sense of helplessness and hopelessness. They typically fail to do something very important: look for a variety of answers to their problems. They tend to drastically constrict their options, usually seeing only two possibilities: getting rid of the problems completely or cutting themselves off from them completely. Their pain and desperation drive out all other options.

A very similar psychological autopsy might have been made for a man named Heman, who lived in a very different time and culture but experienced the same sense of doom. He left us an equally chilling note.

He said he'd been placed in "the lowest pit," "the darkest depths." "You have taken from me my closest friends," he told God, "and have made me repulsive to them." He felt trapped, with no way of escape, utterly abandoned by the Almighty, engulfed by secret terrors, even set apart with those who lie in the grave. Heman's note ended with this ominous statement: "The darkness is my closest friend."

This is the wrenching cry of Psalm 88, the closest thing to a suicide note we have in the Bible and a record of personal torment as moving as anything we might find today scribbled in some lonely hotel room or on the edge of a balcony. At this point in Heman's life, he felt absolutely helpless and hopeless. Death loomed over him, overshadowing all other options.

The tunnel vision that haunts the suicidal is something with which we all have trouble on occasion. At times we feel stuck between a rock and a hard place; the walls start closing in on us; all our choices seem to involve unpleasant possibilities. It's then that we need to look at all the options; we must somehow broaden our horizon. And that requires a measure of hope, an energy inside us that points to the alternatives.

When it seems pointless to go on, when things can't possibly get any worse, we need the language of hope. Fortunately, the psalms provide us with that language in abundance.

Listen to the words of an old, enfeebled King David, besieged by enemies:

> For You have been my hope, O Sovereign Lord,
>   my confidence since my youth.

When Ethan the Ezrahite felt abandoned—"How I bear in my heart the taunts of all the nations"—he determined to speak in terms of hope: "With my mouth I will make your faithfulness known through all generations. I will declare that your love stands firm forever."

One of the sons of Korah reminded himself of what to do when the gloom settles in:

> Why are you downcast, O my soul?
>   Why so disturbed within me?
> Put your hope in God,
>   for I will yet praise him,
>   my Savior and my God.

The author of Psalm 130 resolved to look up in the darkest hour with all the eagerness of a lonely sentry looking for the dawn:

> My soul waits for the Lord
>   more than watchmen wait for the morning,
>   more than watchmen wait for the morning.

And David gives us perhaps the most beautiful picture in the Bible about what hoping in God really means:

> I have stilled and quieted my soul;
>   like a weaned child with its mother,
>   like a weaned child is my soul within me.
> O Israel, put your hope in the Lord
>   both now and forevermore.

This kind of hope is part of the good news of the gospel. We don't have to be chained to the past. No matter how many times we've failed, no matter how badly others have failed us, God is capable of giving us "day one" again.

The Father specializes in new births, new beginnings. He can make the old pass away. And those who begin a relationship with

Him are given again "new birth into a living hope," as Peter tells us. It's this living hope that we need in our moments of despair. A present-tense hope, a hope that affects us right now where we are, can have dramatic results.

When Bill was a senior in high school, he got into the habit of contemplating the meaning of life. As a result he grew somewhat suicidal. It was the usual idealism of youth grinding against the usual disasters in the world. At times it hardly seemed worth pursuing an education or a career—or even a life—amid all the compromises Bill saw around him. He'd been exposed in school to the prevailing ideas of values-free acceptance. But he couldn't bring himself to just accept. It was a lie to accept evil, a lie to say that things were OK.

So Bill began toying with the idea of ending it all. But then, in the middle of his gloomy reflections, a thought lighted up in his head: If there was just one person who lived a good life, a completely good life, it would be worth it all. He'd seen plenty of evidence that even the best of humanity hid pockets of cruelty. But what if there was an exception? That would made a difference.

Bill carried that thought around for a while as his last argument against suicide. Then he spent a holiday at his aunt's house. She was a Christian woman, and she reminded him of his days in Sunday School. All those stories about Jesus came back to him. Truths that he'd stuck away in the back of his mind since childhood awakened inside him, and suddenly he realized that this was his answer, exactly. Jesus was the completely good Man who made life worthwhile. That became just a little island of hope in the middle of his gloomy world. Bill found a reason to live, something that loomed larger in his mind than all the problems he saw around him.

I'm glad Bill didn't sink into terminal tunnel vision. Otherwise I would never have had the privilege of knowing this great friend in college.

Faithfulness springs from the earth

The language of hope helps us break through the walls of despair when life seems to close in with equally bleak alternatives. But the question is, How do we get there from here? What is this hope based on? How are we motivated to speak that language? It may help to step back and look at what lies beyond the darkest hours of our life.

It usually starts with a sense of disappointment; a shadow creeps over your life. Then a feeling of weariness settles in. Every little act takes enormous effort. People try to cheer you up. But somehow you feel shut away from everyone; you withdraw further and further into a numbing shell. The author of Psalm 31 expressed that sense of isolation graphically:

> I am a dread to my friends. . . .
> I am forgotten by them as though I were dead;
> I have become like broken pottery.

You try to fight this dominating gloom and desperately look for some way out, but the sense of dejection saps all your energy. Sometimes it can make you physically sick:

> I am feeble and utterly crushed. . . .
> I am like a deaf man, who cannot hear,
> like a mute, who cannot open his mouth. . . .
> My pain is ever with me.

The dark extends out too far on every side. And you sink deeper into the apparently bottomless pit that is—depression. The psalmist knew all about it:

> The waters have come up to my neck.
> I sink in the miry depths,
> where there is no foothold.

Researchers have recently concluded that depression produces more human suffering than any other disease that afflicts us. Health professionals estimate that untreated cases of depression reach as high as four to eight million annually in the United States.

People who pen those suicide notes are obviously laboring under a heavy case of the blues. If we are able to find a detour around those darkest hours of life, we must first deal with the gloomy mind-set that creates that downward spiral in the first place.

Depression can generally be traced to some loss we've experienced—loss of a loved one, job opportunity, or self-esteem. It's essentially a reaction to loss, a sense of disappointment.

Christian counselor Dr. Tim LaHaye has broken down the blues into certain components. You start with a loss or disappointment; then you add another essential ingredient: resentment and anger. You keep thinking how wrongly you were treated and how unfair life has been. You resent what's happened; anger builds within.

Then comes the third element: all this is multiplied by self-pity. Self-pity multiplies sadness into gloom. Our lot in life begins to appear unbearable. The loss, the disappointment, grows larger and larger. Prospects for a solution grow smaller and smaller. We get caught up in a sorrow that seems endless, like the author of Psalm 6:

> I am worn out from groaning;
>> all night long I flood my bed with weeping
>> and drench my couch with tears.
> My eyes grow weak with sorrow.

This, then, is the formula: You take a loss, add resentment, multiply by self-pity, and come out with a guaranteed case of the blues. LOSS + RESENTMENT x SELF-PITY = DEPRESSION.

So what we need to do is break that faulty thought pattern in order to disarm depression. We need a counterweight to our usual resentment response. That counterweight is God's grace, an awareness of His favor. Listen to how this idea is expressed in Psalm 85:

> I will listen to what God the Lord will say;
>> he promises peace to his people, his saints—
>> but let them not return to folly.
> Surely his salvation is near those who fear him,
>> that his glory may dwell in our land.
> Love and faithfulness meet together;
>> righteousness and peace kiss each other.
> Faithfulness springs forth from the earth,
>> and righteousness looks down from heaven.
> The Lord will indeed give what is good,
>> and our land will yield its harvest.

Grace may seem like an exclusively New Testament concept, but it does form a theme in the Old Testament and especially in the Psalms. Usually the idea is expressed by the word *lovingkindness*. This is Yahweh's covenant love for His people. But it's not just a concept; it becomes a living thing, a living environment in the eyes of the psalmist. God's faithfulness is something that blossoms out of the earth like a vine full of grapes. His righteousness hovers over us like a beaming cloud. His glory actually takes up residence in the land. Thus embedded in the psalmist's world, these divine qualities become beneficently active, meeting and embracing like soul mates. All this is the writer's way of expressing the fact that God will indeed bestow what is good. His will is to bless us.

This is grace. And the psalmist has come to realize that he actually lives and moves and has his being *in* God's grace, His lovingkindness. We discover an echo of this mind-set in the experience of Paul, whose letter to the Philippians demonstrates how he was able to keep rejoicing in that most depressing of predicaments: imprisonment. Paul wasn't just *in* a dungeon; he was *in* God's grace. That divine regard surrounded him.

So here's our alternative to resentment: instead of brooding over the loss, we point our predicament heavenward. We reaffirm the fact that we don't just live in this problem; we also live in God's grace. He wants the best for us; He will work to make something good come out of an unfortunate loss.

But after adding grace, we need to multiply by a third element: thankfulness. Paul exemplifies this quality wonderfully in Philippians. And the psalms (as we shall see in the next chapter) are full of thanksgiving. Casting about for what we have to be thankful for is a wonderful antidote to self-pity. It's all a matter of what you choose to look at. As you verbalize your thanks to God, you'll find that His grace multiplies inside you.

So now we have a way to short-circuit the old formula of loss plus resentment multiplied by self-pity producing depression. Instead, we add the new perspective of grace and expand it with expressions of gratitude to the God of lovingkindness. We have a new formula: LOSS + GRACE x THANKFULNESS = PEACE.

This is what we can do when the blues threaten to seep in and set up housekeeping. And this is how we are inspired to echo the

language of hope. Our hope is not just a whistling in the dark. We
hope because God's grace is all around us, beaming down from
heaven, blossoming up from the earth, embracing us as God's own.

Close to the brokenhearted

We've seen that depression is the road that leads us into the most
despairing moments of life. Now let's try to step back from depression and uncover its roots. Often they go far back to something that
happened in the distant past.

Maybe it happened a long, long time ago. You wanted so badly
to belong. But "they" wouldn't let you. There's a hurt there that
time doesn't always erase. You still feel the scars:

> They have greatly oppressed me from my youth. . . .
> Plowmen have plowed my back
>   and made their furrows long.

Maybe it happened when life was just beginning to blossom. You
thought that love had come to the rescue at last and you would live
happily ever after. But then you were suddenly, inexplicably
rejected. You were not wanted. That pain still cuts deep:

> Look to my right and see;
>   no one is concerned for me.
> I have no refuge;
>   no one cares for my life.

And you also found that the more you tried to hide that old
wound inside, the worse it festered, poisoning your relationships,
sabotaging your self-esteem. What a terrible hole that tragedy
leaves inside you! It seems that nothing can ever fill it, nothing ever
make up for this consuming hurt.

> When I was silent and still,
>   not even saying anything good,
>   my anguish increased.
> My heart grew hot within me,
>   and as I meditated, the fire burned.

In many different times and in many different ways, we are wounded—sometimes just bruised, sometimes cut deeply, sometimes hurt to the depths, but we all bear scars of one kind or another. And all of us are left with one big question: "Will I ever find real healing?"

Does God really heal—on the inside, where it matters most? That's an important question in our scar-intensive world. We do occasionally hear stories of miraculous physical healing—someone's crippled legs are straightened, or someone's malignant tumor suddenly disappears. But what about a different kind of affliction, what about all those who suffer in heart and mind and soul?

Festering emotional wounds are what make us most vulnerable to depression. The usual bumps and bruises of daily life don't drag us down too badly if we're buoyed up by a sense of love and acceptance. But when some hurt in the past keeps opening up, those daily problems can shove us right back down in the hole again.

Christian physician and counselor Dr. Paul Tournier once made a remarkable discovery. It happened when he encountered "the greatest despair . . . I have ever met in my career as a doctor." It involved a young woman named Emma who had lost the one consolation of her unhappy life; her young daughter had been killed. She was inconsolable in her grief, shouting, cursing, and striking herself. Tournier remained with this woman for several hours but was unable to get a word in. He did speak to Emma's Christian aunt, though, and encouraged her to bring Emma to the God who could heal.

The possibility of healing for this bereaved mother seemed terribly remote. She expressed intense anger, hostility, and bitterness, blaming God for the tragedy. But the aunt stuck by her, showing kindness and understanding. After a while, Emma allowed the woman to pray with her. This aunt continued talking to her about God and what He could offer.

And somehow this despairing mother found her way to healing. In fact, she came to believe that consecrating her life to God was the only way to deal with her grief and the void in her heart. So Emma did so. And a month later, friends listened in awe as she spoke of finding genuine happiness, despite her sorrow, because she had found God.

Hard evidence exists that God can and does heal our deepest wounds. If many of the psalms reflect deeply wounded hearts, many also speak of deeply felt healing. The psalmists confidently praise the God who "heals the brokenhearted and binds up their wounds." These writers speak from experience when they declare:

> The Lord is close to the brokenhearted
> and saves those who are crushed in spirit.

After David's narrow escape from "going down into the pit," he could affirm, "O Lord my God, I called to you for help and you healed me." When he confessed that "my heart is wounded within me. I fade away like an evening shadow," he was also able to acknowledge that his Lord "stands at the right hand of the needy one."

It is evident in the psalms that the God who "heals all [your] diseases" heals the afflictions of the soul. He does touch our deepest wounds with His skillful hands. He can heal so well because He was deeply wounded Himself and bears the scars of all our ordeals in His body. In the heart-wrenching words of Psalm 22, we see a graphic description of Christ's sufferings on the Cross, a remarkable prophecy. Here is a man utterly forsaken by God and despised and insulted by men. His heart is melting like wax; all his bones are out of joint. He dies of thirst while bystanders cast lots for his clothing. He is poured out like water while lions roar around him.

Yes, God knows all about rejection. He does not stand aloof from our pain. He knows all about being cut off from those closest to Him. He knows all about suffering unjustly.

Can God touch your pain? Yes, He already has, all of it. He knows what it's like to be a victim. He absorbed the guilt of child molesters, thieves, rapists, abusive parents, warmongers, drug pushers . . . He took it all at Golgotha. On the cross, Jesus was crushed beneath the weight of all these tragedies and all that pain.

God's grace is an environment in which we may live. His good will toward us can help disarm depression. But through the cross, that grace has become more; it's a hand reaching inside us, touching our deepest wounds. God can heal us because He can feel with us. He knows more profoundly than we can imagine all the hurt inside us. He knows just the right balm for our wounds.

And this is the ultimate reason why we may speak the language of hope in the darkest hours. God is there with us. With Him at our side, there's always a way out.

Chapter 5
The Solution Is Thanks

Let the redeemed say this

They are like a succession of scenes from "Rescue 911": travelers who were dying of thirst in desert wastelands are led to a city where they find food and water; prisoners languishing in chains see gates of bronze broken down before them; those who've collapsed after gorging themselves sick are helped; people caught in a tempest, staggering around like drunken men as waves tower over them, suddenly behold the wind calm and the sea grow still.

All these remarkable adventures are recorded in Psalm 107, a liturgical narrative that presents Yahweh as the chief protagonist: the great rescuer. And the point of this psalm is repeated four times in its refrain:

> Let them give thanks to the Lord for his unfailing love
>   and his wonderful deeds for men.

Interwoven through scores of psalms is a bright, energetic language, the language of thanksgiving, which forms one of the great themes of this longest book of Scripture.

The theme overflows in Psalm 147, where the author is brim-filled with reasons to thank the One who heals the brokenhearted, numbers the stars, and fructifies the earth. That overflowing becomes musical:

> Sing to the Lord with thanksgiving;
>   make music to our God on the harp.

In Psalm 116, that same emotion reaches a new intensity as the writer ponders how gracious, righteous, and full of compassion God has been toward him. The psalmist has just been rescued from the cords of death:

> How can I repay the Lord
>> for all his goodness to me?

He vows to make a sacrifice of thanksgiving to this God.

Other psalmists speak during more peaceful days, but as they count their blessings, they speak the same language:

> Lord, you have assigned me my portion and my cup;
>> you have made my lot secure.
> The boundary lines have fallen for me in pleasant places;
>> surely I have a delightful inheritance.

Speaking of himself in the third person as the king, David gratefully declares:

> You have granted him the desire of his heart
>> and have not withheld the request of his lips.

From the breathless sense of deliverance in Psalm 116 to the mellowed devotion of Psalm 147; from the short burst of Psalm 100, shouting with joy, to the long narrative of Psalm 107, listing God's great rescues, thanksgiving permeates the psalms.

And we are urged to participate in that experience. Psalm 107, the great anthem of thanksgiving, opens with these words:

> Give thanks to the Lord, for he is good;
>> his love endures forever.
> Let the redeemed of the Lord say this.

In other words, don't just sit there listening to these lofty words; get involved, say it, express thanks. In order for it to do you much good, you have to make it your own idiom.

This is one of the most useful languages you could ever learn. And the settings in which you can practice it are endless.

Giving thanks benefits us, first of all, because it is inherently an expansive language. It opens up a wider horizon before our eyes, new possibilities to our minds. Listen to the author of Psalm 95:

> Let us come before him with thanksgiving
>   and extol him with music and song.
> For the Lord is the great God,
>   the great King above all gods.
> In his hand are the depths of the earth,
>   and the mountain peaks belong to him.
> The sea is his, for he made it,
>   and his hands formed the dry land.

Aiming our appreciation at the King of the universe, who holds all things in the palm of His hand, naturally nudges us out of whatever rut we've been complaining or worrying or fuming in. There's a bigger world out there in which God is active.

Giving thanks expands us; it opens us up. And that's one of the prerequisites to learning. People who practice thanks are more able to absorb new things. Let me give you a specific example of how thanksgiving can actually help you learn.

First, think about something you are least likely to be grateful for. How about teenagers? My older brother once remarked, only half-jokingly, that all people between twelve and twenty should be herded together and confined to some camp in New Jersey (he lives in California). We're all used to hearing about the hassles of that rebellious coming of age. Teenagers are just old enough to reason for themselves but not yet quite reasonable—passionate about freedom, yet fumble-fingered about responsibility. When it comes to lodging complaints, teenagers are an easy target.

But remember the time Jesus stopped His disciples cold when they wanted to hurry away the toddlers who had been brought for His blessing? He spoke of them as the first citizens of the kingdom. Those quarrelsome disciples had something to learn from the children's guileless humility. Maybe God also has something for us to learn from teenagers. A little thankfulness can open our eyes.

Have you ever thought of being thankful that teenagers rarely worry? Most of the time we see this in terms of a failure to take life seriously. Kids find it so easy to forget all about the problems that inundate their parents. Nothing bothers them. Shrugging seems to be the quintessential teenage response to life's challenges. But maybe shrugging isn't all bad. Jesus once asked those struggling for life's basic necessities to consider the lilies and sparrows, concluding: "Do not be anxious for tomorrow; for tomorrow will care for itself."

Worry tends to absorb energy without producing anything—it's a mental running in place. As one writer put it, "Most worries are reruns." There comes a time when we all must stop and just trust.

Youthful "irresponsibility" may be a needed corrective for our "mature" worry. Teenagers tend to enjoy the present moment fully. Small pleasures captivate them more easily. They are free to dangle bare feet in the stream of everyday adventure.

While I was attending a boarding academy in south Texas, a hurricane swept up the coast from the Gulf of Mexico. Winds of 150 mph were predicted for our area. Parents made frantic phone calls. The faculty prepared for the worst. A couple of teachers fled upstate. But the kids had a ball.

When the storm came, we watched enthralled as roofs unraveled and an old frame building imploded. Since our campus was inundated, we went canoeing over to the girls' dorm and back, then played outrageous games of football in two feet of water.

It was good that parents were concerned and that the faculty prayed. But also valuable was our "immature" capacity to enjoy the storm and to have the time of our lives in its aftermath.

Remember to thank God for teenagers; they often remind us of lilies and sparrows in a world of bills and deadlines.

And they do something else. When teens turn to Christ, they often do so with refreshing zeal. The light that hits them has kick, and they feel compelled to do something about it. I remember well the earnest, glowing faces of kids giving their testimonies at youth retreats. The power of that first flash of dedication is hard to recapture.

Teenagers seem to commit themselves with a purer devotion. Their whole lives are ahead of them; hopes and dreams have not given way to cynical disclaimers. They have a lot to lay at Jesus' feet. It's a bigger gift and makes a bigger splash.

Those of us who've settled down, spiritually and otherwise, often find it hard to share the spontaneous praises of the young. Maturity has taught us to cover our tracks and avoid burning bridges behind us. Loyalty is not so simple anymore—we keep one eye on the pearly gates and the other on prevailing interest rates.

So thank God for teenagers and the fire of their first love. It may burn erratically for a while, but it may also help us to sing that "new song" the psalms are always talking about. It may help us remember that faith involves change and growth. Thank God for kids who've not yet "settled into the truth." Their instability sometimes makes them more malleable in God's hands.

Expanding our circle of thankfulness helps us to learn new things—sometimes from quite unexpected sources.

What thankfulness produces

In narrating that succession of "Rescue 911" scenes, Psalm 107 links thanksgiving with the God who solves problems, all kinds of problems. A panorama of dangers and predicaments is laid out for us in those verses, and God finds a way to extricate His people from every one of them. The psalm's recurring refrain urges us to respond with thanks.

I believe thanksgiving links us in a special way with the problem-solving God. Because our thanks is directed His way, it acquires something of His creative power. If you've got a problem, giving thanks could well be a key part of the solution.

A young woman named Sandra walked into her pastor's office utterly despondent. She began to pour out a long, painful story. Her husband, it seemed, treated her with contempt. Nothing she did pleased him. She dreaded his return from work each day.

Sandra was a very beautiful young woman, but her painful awareness of rejection had turned her into a defeated, frigid, tense wife. And the more she felt of her husband's disdain, the less motivated she became to please him. Sandra was trapped in a vicious cycle. The walls of depression were closing in.

So the pastor decided to meet with Sandra's husband. Joe was quite amazed when he heard that he was the key to his wife's depression. Like most men, he didn't understand how well his wife could read his attitude. The pastor suggested that Joe do one specific thing: "Select ten positive qualities in your wife," he said, "and thank God for them. Thank God twice a day, in the morning and on the way home from work."

That didn't seem terribly difficult, so Joe agreed. He began thanking God for things he liked about Sandra. And before long, she began to change. She became more relaxed and affectionate. Joe continued to be thankful, and Sandra grew in self-respect and motivation. She broke out of the walls of her depression.

Later the pastor asked Joe if he had memorized his list of ten positive qualities. "I not only have it memorized," Joe replied, "but I'm finding new things in her to be grateful for every day."

Thankfulness produces thankfulness. It's a powerful force in human life, not just an escape from life's harsher realities. It isn't just a vague spiritual exercise; it's a solution. Take the problem of chronic fear, for example.

For the first time in her life, Patricia found herself alone over long periods. Her husband had taken a position with his church that required him to travel extensively—often for weeks at a time. Patricia had always been a people-person, happily wrapped up in her family, mothering her three daughters through the ups and downs of adolescence. But now they had all married and moved away. And now her husband, too, was increasingly absent.

Patricia found herself sitting alone at home, night after night, wondering what purpose she had anymore. And there was fear to contend with—all the things that go through a woman's mind as she tries to sleep in an empty house.

Well, Patricia realized that if she didn't get a hold of her fears, they would inflate out of control. She had to have something else to fasten her mind on. And so she turned to that God celebrated in the psalms as the sure shelter and strong tower and everlasting arms. She asked God to give her some clear purpose she could cling to—even in an empty house. And the Lord answered.

Patricia realized, very forcefully, that she could either become a complaining, nervous woman, focused on her loneliness, or she could accept her situation and reach out cheerfully toward others—even when her husband was gone. Patricia saw this as a new role that God was giving her at this point in her life. She would willingly give up her husband to his work for the church rather than moan about it. And she could bless other people in the process.

Patricia found a way out of suffocating fears by fastening her thoughts on a purpose she felt God was giving her. She was able to focus on this new calling by thanking God for it.

Patricia's solution might be very different from what someone else might be given in similar circumstances. But the point is, she found a positive direction for her thoughts, an alternative to dwelling on the loneliness and fear. And it happened because this woman began to express thanks for the new role she could play.

When actress Helen Hays was a girl just starting out in the theater, she would hear people murmuring prayers, often panicky prayers, just before the curtain went up. Everyone seemed to be asking for something, and Helen worried that perhaps no one ever thought to send up a prayer of thanks to God. So after a rehearsal one afternoon she rushed back to her room and wrote out her own prayer of thanksgiving.

She recollected years later, "I was sure God would be so grateful to receive it, amid all the prayers asking for help, that he would do something wonderful for the world."

Helen eventually lost that prayer, but the sentiment has stayed with her. As she looks out the window of her home on the Hudson River at all the glorious shapes and colors, the language comes back: "Not a day passes that I forget to whisper thanks."

And Helen Hays has found that thanks helps her deal with the losses that have come in her life. "When my husband, Charlie, died, I found peace and strength reading the Psalms—the same ones we had read over and over in the hard months of our daughter Mary's illness and subsequent death." The language of thanksgiving helped this woman through the grieving process. The words of the poets and prophets became "steadfast friends whom I have called upon for comfort."

Thanksgiving does help us grapple with real problems in the real world. There is nothing that can have a more positive impact on our emotional well-being than a spirit of thankfulness. The psalms can teach us that essential language of the heart.

When I put on sackcloth

The author of Psalm 69 felt that he'd sunk into the miry depths without a foothold, become engulfed in a flood, and grown hoarse from calling for help—in vain. People made fun of him when he put on sackcloth. And yet even in that pit of pain and distress he made this resolve:

> I will praise God's name in song
>   and glorify him with thanksgiving.

We can glorify God even in our darkest hour. How? By giving thanks. That is one of the highest experiences we can have while living on this planet dominated by sin and tragedy. We have to dig down deeper into our hearts for those words that circumstances can't erase. The surest way of expressing the fact that we do belong to a separate kingdom is the giving of thanks when there seems no earthly reason to do so. That's when the language of thanksgiving is noblest and its witness most powerful.

As the head of Prison Fellowship International, Ron Nikkel has visited prisons in over fifty countries. He works to share the message of Christ with inmates and labors with governments to improve prison conditions. Ron has seen institutions of horrifying brutality and institutions intent on reform; he's seen men at their worst—and at their best.

In jails around the world, Ron Nikkel has discovered the ultimate testing ground of forgiveness and love and grace. And surprisingly enough, he has seen the strongest evidence of a living Christ in the faces of men who were once hardened criminals.

A journalist once asked Ron to tell him about the worst prison he'd ever seen. The reporter wondered if he'd ever been to a place so fearful, so despairing, as to crush any signs of faith or hope. What place had been the ultimate test of the gospel?

Ron thought for a moment and then began describing a 1986 visit to a maximum-security prison in Zambia. While there he'd learned of a secret inner prison built to hold the most dangerous offenders. To Ron's amazement, one of the guards agreed to let him into the facility so he could speak a few words to the men.

They proceeded through dark corridors and giant steel doors to a cagelike building covered with wire mesh. Cells built into the outside of the cage surrounded a small courtyard. The prisoners were allowed to walk around the courtyard only one hour a day.

The rest of the time they were confined to cells so small and crowded that the men could not all lie down at once.

When the last gate into the inner prison swung open, Ron gasped in the foul, stifling atmosphere. He had never seen squalor like this. There were no sanitation facilities; prisoners had to relieve themselves wherever they could. The blazing African sun was heating up the steel enclosure unbearably. Ron could hardly breathe. He wondered how human beings could exist in such a place. Surely, of all places in the world, fear and despair would prove overwhelming here.

But something remarkable happened as soon as Ron was introduced to the inmates. Eighty of the 120 prisoners quietly filed to the back wall and assembled themselves in rows. And then they began singing hymns. They sang words of Christian praise and thanksgiving beautifully, in four-part harmony. Ron's companion whispered that thirty-five of these men had been sentenced to death and would soon face execution.

Later, Ron Nikkel would recall the scene in this way: "I was overwhelmed by the contrast between their peaceful, serene faces and the horror of their surroundings. Just behind them, in the darkness, I could make out an elaborate charcoal sketch drawn on the wall. It showed Jesus, stretched out on the cross. And it struck me with great force that Christ was there with them. He was sharing their suffering and giving them joy enough to sing in such a place."

Ron was supposed to speak to the men, sharing words of encouragement. But awed by their faith, he could only mumble a few words of greeting. He felt they were the teachers, not he.

Thanksgiving brings Christ close, even in the darkest, most fearful places. That's where this language shines brightest. Even in a pit of suffocating despair, our words of thanks can lift up Christ as He stretches out His arms. Like a charcoal sketch on the wall, He is a very present comforter in our hearts.

Chapter 6
When Church Gets Boring

Like precious oil poured out

The bus from Tel Aviv rumbled along on Israel's semifreeways and headed toward the hills surrounding Jerusalem. Like the other tourist-pilgrims seated around me, I wanted this moment to register; I wanted to see and feel my entry into the Holy Land. But it was ten at night and raining hard. Nothing much showed out the windows.

Our guide, however, did his best to make the occasion dramatic. He gave us a story explaining why there were so many stones on the side of the road. "All the pilgrims who've carried a lifelong burden to visit the holy city finally get their chance along this ancient path. They drop their burdens like stones, hurry up the last hill, and behold the place of their dreams. Your lifelong dream is about to come true too."

We did round the last hill and pushed our noses against the streaked windowpanes. But all I could make out in the dark was a few lights on the hills, spread as nondescriptly as those of any town.

The next morning, when I woke in our high-rise hotel, I still couldn't make out Jerusalem. It lay somewhere out there in the heavy fog and rain.

So I tried to be philosophical and muse that this was indeed a fitting introduction to our tour. Zion, after all, isn't just the layout of beige stone that appears in wide photographic profile. It's least of all the landmark Dome of the Rock, an impolite Muslim addition to sacred ground. Jerusalem is a place of the imagination, home base

51

for the God of heaven and earth. The only people who really saw the city meaningfully were those trekking over from Jericho and Hebron and Galilee, singing their songs of ascent as they neared the place of Passover, Feast of Tabernacles, and Pentecost, the place of Yahweh's temple. I tried to imagine what it was like for them.

On the hills near Bethlehem, dusty shepherds and their families traveling east from Gath met up with several farmer clans coming down from Gibeah. The shepherds had a few lambs among them, and the farmers brought sheaves of wheat. As the two groups intersected on the road, the shepherds called out:

> I lift up my eyes to the hills—
>   where does my help come from?

The farmers sang back lustily:

> My help comes from the Lord,
>   the maker of heaven and earth.

The pilgrims from Gath smiled broadly and continued in unison:

> He will not let your foot slip—
>   he who watches over you will not slumber.

Walking all together now on the trail, the farmers echoed:

> Indeed, he who watches over Israel
>   will neither slumber nor sleep.

Climbing up the last ridge, the shepherds sang out:

> The Lord watches over you—
>   the Lord is your shade at your right hand.

The others sang with increasing excitement:

> The sun will not harm you by day,
>   nor the moon by night.

Then the group rounded a bend, and the ridge fell away to reveal the City of David shining brightly in the sun, a jewel bordered on all sides by rich green olive and fig trees. The shepherds sang out to the valley below:

> The Lord will keep you from all harm—
>   he will watch over your life.

And their brothers finished the psalm:

> The Lord will watch over your coming and going
>   both now and forevermore.

Now everyone broke into shouts and hallelujahs. There was much slapping of backs, a few embraces; some of the older ones looked at the city with tears in their eyes. And they descended the Mount of Olives, talking happily of the coming festivities, no longer strangers on the road but now a kind of spontaneous family caught up in the sense that their benevolent God had been made visible among them.

Psalm 121 is one in a series (120-134) called "songs of ascent," which worshipers sang on their way to Mount Zion for the annual pilgrimages. This common language created a fellowship, which was celebrated in one of the songs in the series, Psalm 133:

> How good and pleasant it is
>   when brothers live together in unity!
> It is like precious oil poured on the head. . . .
> It is as if the dew of Hermon
>   were falling on Mount Zion.

Once in a while we get a glimpse of how precious that language of spiritual unity really is.

A man from Holland, called simply Brother Andrew, had just smuggled a load of Bibles in his VW across the Romanian border. He checked into a motel and began praying that God would lead him to the right Christian groups—the ones who could best use these copies of the Scriptures. This was the 1950s, a time when

Eastern Europe seemed populated largely by spies and secret police.

On Sunday morning Andrew walked up to the hotel clerk and asked where he might find a church.

The clerk looked at him a little strangely and answered, "We don't have many of those, you know. Besides, you couldn't understand the language."

"Didn't you know," Andrew replied, "Christians speak a kind of universal language?"

"Oh, what's that?"

"It's called Agape."

"Agape?" the clerk wondered. "I've never heard of it."

"Too bad," Andrew replied. "It's the most beautiful language in the world."

Fortunately, Andrew was able to locate several church groups in the area, and he managed to arrange a meeting with the president and secretary of a certain denomination; we'll call them James and Leon. They sat down together in a small office. Andrew was eager to tell them about the Bibles he had smuggled into the country. He also wanted to find out something about the men and their churches. But soon the three discovered that they couldn't speak a word that was understandable.

Andrew knew several European languages, and so did the Romanians. But they had no tongue in common. So there they sat, staring at each other across the room. Andrew had come thousands of dangerous miles in his little VW. He longed to bring greetings and encouragement from Christians in the Western world to these brothers isolated behind the Iron Curtain. But how?

Then Andrew got an idea. He noticed James had a Bible on his desk. Andrew reached into his coat pocket and pulled out a Dutch Bible. He turned to 1 Corinthians 16:20 and held the Bible out, pointing to the name of the book, which they could recognize. Instantly their faces lighted up. They quickly found the same chapter and verse in their Romanian Bibles and read this verse: "All the brothers here send you greetings. Greet one another with a holy kiss."

James and Leon beamed back at Andrew. Then James looked through his Bible and pointed out Proverbs 25:25. Andrew found the verse and read: "Like cold water to a weary soul is good news from a distant land."

By then all three were laughing together. Andrew responded by turning to the book of Philemon. He pointed his brothers to verses 4 and 5. They read: "I always thank my God as I remember you in my prayers, because I hear about your faith in the Lord Jesus and your love for all the saints."

The two Romanians nodded, smiling. Then Leon's eyes wandered down to verse 7. He pushed the Bible over to Andrew, pointing to these beautiful words: "Your love has given me great joy and encouragement, because you, brother, have refreshed the hearts of the saints."

These three men had a wonderful time together. They spent half an hour conversing and sharing—just through the words of Scripture. They were so happy in their fellowship that they laughed until tears came to their eyes.

Finally, Andrew showed his brothers the Bibles he had brought for them. James and Leon were overwhelmed and overjoyed. They embraced him again and again.

That evening, when Andrew returned to his hotel, the clerk approached him and remarked, "Say, I looked up *agape* in the dictionary. There's no language by that name. That's just a Greek word for love."

Andrew replied, "That's it. I was speaking in it all afternoon."

Lift up banners

Most of us have some idea of the benefits of fellowship and communal worship; we do want to speak that heavenly language together. But too often the actual experience of going to church leaves us yawning. We vow to pay attention, for the umpteenth time, but then as the service progresses, our pulse slows in the warm sanctuary, our head nods at the familiar phrases, our eyelids grow heavy, and we wander off into a bemused trickle of thoughts.

Why is worship so boring so often? How can it be made more inspiring?

One important answer is implicit in the book of Psalms. Many of these songs were written to celebrate certain festivals. The "songs of ascent" series is a prime example. These were praises lifted up as pilgrims walked to the holy city or entered into the temple court. The worshipers were involved in a physical coming to God, sometimes involving lengthy exertion, as they exalted His character in song.

Worship for the Hebrews was a participant phenomenon, not some formality that they passively absorbed. Glance through the psalms, and you'll see calls to energetic expression everywhere:

> Play skillfully, and shout for joy.
> Clap your hands, all you nations.
> Let us shout aloud to the Rock.
> Sing to the glory of his name.
> Lift up your hands in the sanctuary.
> Praise him with tambourine and dancing.
> We . . . will lift up our banners in the name of our God.
> I will come and proclaim your mighty acts.

action   *love also is something th.*   *we do.*

Worship was indeed a verb for the Hebrews. In the psalms we see a picture of active, joyful participation in something much bigger and more important than any individual part. Worship happens with every kind of instrument: "Praise him with the sounding of the trumpet . . . harp and lyre . . . clash of cymbals." And every kind of person is involved: "Praise the Lord . . . young men and maidens, old men and children."

It would be well for us to devise worship services that employ more active participation and meaningful expression on the part of those in the pews. Church is boring primarily because it is such a passive, routine experience.

But each of us can do something to change that right now, with whatever kind of service our church happens to use. Let's take the feature of the traditional eleven-o'clock hour that seems least likely to allow audience participation: the sermon.

Facing yet another drowsy service at our tiny church in the hills of western Illinois, I hit on an idea that might keep my nodding family awake. Why not take notes during the sermon and do a little detective work on our own? It could be a kind of game. This time we could jot down every fact mentioned that suggested a reason to thank God. After the service we would compare notes and see who had uncovered the most things to praise God for.

The family went for it. Instead of groaning critically during the long exposition, we found ourselves reflecting on the pastor's theme, connecting various points, turning familiar phrases into original praise.

During the long drive home, we all shared what we'd written down. It was fascinating to see how each person had responded creatively to the sermon. Our detective work paid off. The mention of Nicodemus coming to Jesus by night clued my wife in on the fact that the Lord is available twenty-four hours a day. And the mention of Jesus getting right to the point—"You must be born again"—reminded me to thank Him for the times He has been pointed in my own life.

With all our tidbits put together, we had quite a meal. Instead of slumping in the after-church daze, we were animated with praise and excited about what we had learned in our joint venture with the pastor.

During other Sabbaths I have suggested other ways to play detective in church. Once I imagined that I was trying to describe God to someone who wandered in from Outer Mongolia and had no knowledge of Jesus Christ. My only source of information would be what the pastor shared that day. I had to pick up and expand on any facts that might fill in the Lord's character, writing down word pictures of God on the basis of these clues.

The minister's exposition on Romans 3 proved quite enlightening. Passages thick with theological terms often float right past me. But this time they rang a bell.

This God must be generous, I concluded, since He gives freely to "all who believe." He must be concerned for everyone. That's a good picture to start with.

The words *justify*, *righteousness*, and *redemption* imply that God is deeply concerned with justice and with our moral standing. Yet it also says He manifests grace freely—an interesting combination.

Detective work like this helped turn me from a slouch in the pew into a participant much more capable of singing for joy and lifting up banners to the Lord.

Sing a new song

One instructive phrase that keeps recurring in the worship of the psalms is: "Sing to the Lord a new song." I believe this is another ingredient that can help prevent our worship program from boring those in the pews. The phrase suggests that there is more to church than the comforts of tradition, services that are always the same. It's about more than just finding alternatives to the same old tunes. The practice of singing a new song implies that worship is a present-tense experience. We talk about what is happening right now in our lives. When David found himself freed from that "slimy pit," he expressed gratitude that "he put a new song in my mouth." We don't just repeat the sentiments of our forefathers in the faith. We lift up the name of the Lord because He is our active contemporary.

The psalmists certainly followed their own advice. They weren't content to mouth a few old standbys that had worn a groove in their throats; they kept on writing about God in the present tense, kept on composing new songs, until they had amassed 150 of them, the longest string of chapters in the Bible.

Lifting up a new song to God also implies that it's OK to innovate in our worship; it's OK to try new things. Whatever particular worship style we've settled into wasn't carved into stone on Mount Sinai. We need to keep an ear out for those new songs that wake us up to worship in the present tense.

There is no one proper way for flowers to be; they blossom in a wild assortment of color and shape. Creation bursts with ingenious adaptation, original form, special skills. In fleshing out the richness of the psalms, we ought to take a cue from the richness of nature. Principles are eternal, but styles infinite; there's plenty of room for a variety of expression.

Most people prefer to make their conversations with the Lord quiet and private. Charles Finney thrived on a different kind of prayer. His critics used to say, "It is impossible for him to pray in secret, for he can be heard a half-mile off." Bellowing out one's petitions may indeed seem insincere and offensive, but one man who heard Finney praying off in the woods at a great distance became so convicted by the man's earnestness that he "sought God's face for redemptive grace."

This matter of what is sincere religion and what isn't trips up a lot of people. Some find it impossible to believe that the young lady sighing sweetly about "my lovely, precious Jesus" can be for real. Others look at a man's expressionless defense of the faith and conclude he hasn't got much religion. Some balk at oratorical heights; others question the plain-spoken.

Christian people get wrapped up in great battles over style—such as whether we should raise our hands in worship or not. The person who sits quietly can't imagine how someone can worship God while making a big commotion. And the person who raises his hands and shouts can't imagine how anyone can worship God motionless in a pew.

When we condemn other styles, we're really assuming that so-and-so can't be for real because we couldn't naturally express our faith that way. But of course different personalities react in different ways to the same truth.

In Christian history there's almost always been pressure to confine worship to one dimension, one style. At one time extemporaneous prayer in public worship was scandalous; you had to go by the book. The saints used to believe that singing anything except psalms in church was an insult to God. Let's face it; conventional religion draws an awful lot of stupid battle lines.

How much better to reveal all the richness of God's character to the world! He is profound Peace, so meditative music expresses something about Him. He is also unbounded Power, so energetic music says something equally valid. Why narrow our picture of God by insisting that only one kind of worship (expressing one sliver of life) is correct? Let a thousand flowers blossom—enough to fill up the world!

During the blustery autumn of 1981, a typhoon brought an unusual amount of rain and wind through our mission compound in Yokohama, Japan. I had become used to "typhoon warnings" as little more than forecasts of precipitation. But this time there was a real storm up. The rain poured down. The trees were jerking about like groupies at a rock concert. The gale actually sheared off a few limbs.

It was then I thought of my buddy Scott, a fellow missionary with whom I could share my struggles and joys. I suggested we go out and enjoy the weather—with a football. We donned our worst clothing and ventured out. The wind rushed us; we had to lean and twirl through it and push through sheets of rain. But those elements were exhilarating. We felt caught up in the unbounded storm. The grass was slick with water. We slipped and slid through two-man tackle football until laughter sapped all our strength.

After resting in the pelting rain, we rose and began leaping and shouting in the storm. The raw elements had never seemed so articulate before. They spoke to us of an energetic God whom no one could ever box in or tie down or sum up. He would always be the Most High over all the earth, dwelling in the height of heaven, a free spirit, uncontainable, full of surprises. Scott and I began shouting Hallelujah at the top of our lungs, joining in with the roar of the wind as leaves and twigs flew past us. The trees shook wildly. It was like a scene from Psalms 96 and 98, in which the sea roars, rivers clap their hands, the fields exult, the mountains and trees sing together for joy, because the Lord, the God who wields nature as a shimmering sword, is coming to rescue His people.

The two of us probably looked rather foolish, but as the trees shook mightily all around, we felt propelled by the same force. The whole earth was alive—every leaf, every blade of grass, wildly animated. We could barely contain the life bursting inside us. And I don't think I have ever worshiped with such abandon.

Chapter 7
Outmaneuvering Our Habits

Chaff vs. fruitful trees

A story is told about Leonardo da Vinci and his painting *The Last Supper*. The artist took some time in locating a model for the face of Christ; he had a hard time finding anyone who exhibited something of the Master's purity and nobility. But at last, looking on the beaming face of a young chorister singing praises in one of the churches of Rome, he knew he'd found his man and proceeded to paint the lovely features of Pietro Bandinelli.

Years passed, and the masterpiece was still uncompleted. All the disciples had been done except Judas Iscariot. Leonardo wanted to find a face that would stand in stark contrast to the countenance of Christ blessing the bread and wine. He searched for a man whose face was hardened and distorted by sin—and eventually found a beggar on the streets of the city whose visage was so villainous that he shuddered to look at it. The beggar sat for Leonardo and became Judas, glancing darkly over at Jesus.

After completing this portrait, the artist said, "I have not yet found out your name."

The scarred beggar pointed up at the canvas and replied, "I am Pietro Bandinelli; I also sat for you as your model of Christ."

Scripture's great book of poetry can be seen as one long canvas on which can be found two faces, two faces as strikingly different as the before-and-after portraits of Bandinelli. The psalms picture the wicked and the righteous in their most cursed and blessed poses;

these figures become stark signs set against the horizon that point toward both what we must flee from and what we must pursue.

Interspersed through the familiar praises of the psalms is an underlying moral voice, a subtheme of uncompromising conviction. It is a voice designed to raise our consciousness about moral choices and to remove the middle ground from beneath our feet.

In the psalms, the wicked aren't just people with a few unfortunate weaknesses who wander off the path a few steps. They strut about, honoring what is vile. The poison of vipers is on their lips; they shoot from the shadows at the upright in heart. They close up their calloused hearts and snarl like dogs prowling about the city.

In the psalms, sin isn't just a matter of missing the mark a bit or failing to live up to certain lofty standards. Sin is cannibalism, the devouring of human beings "as men eat bread." It is to become corrupt, doing nothing good.

The psalmists read the world in black and white, a high-contrast photo focused on the opposite destinies of the righteous and the wicked. The very first psalm introduces this point of view. There the wicked are snapshot as chaff that the wind blows away, while the righteous are pictured as fruitful trees growing by a stream.

In later psalms, disaster hunts down men of violence, but the Lord watches over the way of the righteous. Evildoers testify that they've been plowed over, their bones scattered at the mouth of the grave. The righteous, however, "will still bear fruit in old age, they will stay fresh and green." The unjust are doomed to melt away like slugs crawling along or like a stillborn child who never sees the light of day. The faithful flourish in the courts of God.

This moral voice of the psalms can sound rather harsh at first. But there are occasions in our lives when we badly need to listen to this graphic language. Think about your struggles with an old habit that just won't let go, for example. Frequently, when tempted, we will tell ourselves, very quietly, that this is just a little misstep, no big deal. We just want to take this quick detour and bounce right back on the straight and narrow. We want time out from righteousness, a little break.

But of course that's the same old excuse our habits always make: just this once—week after week, year after year. As Samuel Johnson said, "The chains of habit are generally too small to be felt until they are too strong to be broken." C. S. Lewis wrote in *The Screwtape Letters*: "The safest road to hell is the gradual one—the gentle slope, soft underfoot, without sudden turnings, without milestones, without signposts."

The black-and-white language of the psalms can give us a lift when we start to slip-slide away into old habits. We grab this assumption that it doesn't matter so much and drag it out of the closet. The truth we must challenge it with is this: Two paths diverge at my feet; I have to make a choice about whom to serve. Our action directs us down one of two roads:

> The path of the righteous [uncompromisingly just]
>   is like the first gleam of dawn,
>   shining ever brighter till the full light of day.
> But the way of the wicked is like deep darkness;
>   they do not know what makes them stumble.

We must make our choice very clear, no fudging over a few missteps. We're either following the ever-brighter way of righteousness, or we're stumbling down toward the deep dark.

Many passages in the psalms attempt to make us look beyond this present temptation. What does it lead to? What is the end result? God is not going to cancel our ticket to heaven every time we take a sinful detour, but He does want us to concentrate on what our action says, what direction it points toward. Here's Joshua reflecting that theme as he urged the Hebrews to renew their covenant to Jehovah at Shechem. He said, "'If serving the Lord seems undesirable to you, then choose for yourselves this day whom you will serve, whether the gods your forefathers served beyond the River, or the gods of the Amorites, in whose land you are living. But as for me and my household, we will serve the Lord.'"

Joshua was saying, "If you're not willing to follow God completely, then face the alternatives; you're either going to be serving the moon-god Nanna or Egypt's golden calf or Apis the sacred bull or bloodthirsty Baal and Ashtoreth, demanding the sacrifice of children. Look at the choice you're making."

That's what Scripture pushes us toward. No fuzzy thinking about a little time off from the straight and narrow. Look at the alternatives; you're going to be serving the devil or serving the Lord. Make your choice.

So in response to temptation, we can say: You want me to indulge a bit here? Really? You want me to serve the evil one, who'd like to put an iron yoke about my neck, the one who longs for the day when he can shut me out in his darkness, weeping and gnashing my teeth?

Drag out assumptions and blast them with hard light from the Word. As you do this , the old thought patterns that greased your way into sin will reshape into new radicalized thought patterns that look down the road and fasten on that vision of a life growing brighter and brighter until the "full light of day."

Truth in the inner parts

The psalms do more than just raise our consciousness about sin and righteousness. They also present a way to deal with the sense of failure that inevitably follows this sharpened awareness. In traditional Christian usage, there are seven "penitential psalms." These show us how to be honest with God about our shortcomings.

Notice exactly what happens in these prayers. In Psalm 32, David says, "I acknowledged my sin to you and did not cover up my iniquity. . . . And you forgave the guilt of my sin." In Psalm 38, David talks about his feelings of guilt and terrible distress—and again says simply: "I confess my iniquity." And in Psalm 51, the classic document of confession, he admits, "Against you, you only, have I sinned."

The author of Psalm 130 acknowledges:

> If you, O Lord, kept a record of sins,
> O Lord, who could stand?
> But with you there is forgiveness;
> therefore you are feared.

The psalmists honestly and openly admit their failure to God. They don't moan on and on about the sin they've committed. People often approach the act of confession as a task of persuading God to bestow forgiveness. They give reasons, excuses, present their frailty, explain how sorry they are, and hope that the divine will is thus nudged toward pardon. The feeling is that one must create forgiveness *de novo*, out of nothing. It doesn't exist yet, but our earnest petition may bring it into being.

This attitude places too much weight (and credit) on our act of confession and repentance. We must avoid turning confession into some kind of mini-atonement in which we try to make up for our wrong before God. The fact is, all the really hard work has already been done. Forgiveness, pardon, and justification have been chiseled out for us through Christ's blood, sweat, and tears. Slain on the cross as the spotless Lamb, Christ took on transgressions and created forgiveness—*de novo*. It does not exist apart from Christ's sacrificial act.

So confession is not talking God into something; it's not a sales job. That would be like trying to persuade Michelangelo to repaint the Sistine Chapel ceiling every time we walk in and look up. We have to first believe that the masterpiece is finished; nothing can be added to the forgiveness that the spotless Lamb has already laid out for us in the larger-than-life scene of Golgotha. What we must do is claim it as a great vault of spectacular mercy that covers us right now, as we are, with this messy sin all over our hands.

The Greek word used in the New Testament for *confession* has a root meaning of "assent," "agreement." We agree with God in confession. In Psalm 51, David acknowledged how important honesty and transparency are: "Surely you desire truth in the inner parts; you teach me wisdom in the inmost place." His most earnest pleas were directed at renewal: "Create in me a pure heart . . . renew a steadfast spirit within me." He did not try to talk God into bestowing the forgiveness that He'd already promised.

Keeping in mind exactly who is receiving our confession makes a big difference. A God who cherishes us is listening earnestly. He is the One quite eager to throw our transgressions into the chasms of the sea. There is nothing in the universe that can separate us from His lovingkindness. We make good confession to fulfill God's love, not appease His anger.

Keeping the face of God in mind as we confess will help us open up more easily and more honestly in prayer. The Father whose love is higher than the heavens is also the Lord who sees into our innermost being. Nothing is hidden from His sight. That's important to remember.

Persuading God to forgive us lends itself to the excuses and sleights of habit that hide the real problem. But agreeing with Someone who both loves us infinitely and knows us intimately should help us to be honest. After a lifetime of helping clients with a myriad of ailments come to such an open encounter with God, Dr. Paul Tournier could write: "Christian confession . . . leads to the same psychological liberation as the best psychoanalytical techniques."

Confession can be an enormous sigh of relief: I am responsible; no more games. If we're approaching a God who loves us a great deal, we should have the security to open up a great deal—and receive His forgiveness completely.

Make straight your way

After we've made our honest and open agreement with God about our moral failure, we need to find a way to keep from repeating that failure. We need, as David said, "a steadfast spirit" implanted within us. The psalms themselves communicate that kind of zeal. They do so primarily through proverbs; yes, there are quite a few proverbs in the psalms. They might be called proverb-resolutions, since they typically are made in terms of a personal, heartfelt vow.

That's part of the distinctive heart-language of the psalms. Where Proverbs advises from a distance, Psalms vows up close. Where Proverbs speaks in general terms about principles, Psalms affirms in personal terms about life.

Proverbs solemnly warns of men who "leave the straight paths to walk in dark ways." Psalms calls to the Lord: "Make straight your way before me."

Proverbs declares that "the lamp of the Lord searches the spirit of a man." Psalms responds with a plea:

> Search me, O God, and know my heart;
>   test me and know my anxious thoughts.
> See if there is any offensive way in me,
>   and lead me in the way everlasting.   AMEN!

Proverbs preaches that "he who pursues evil goes to his death." Psalms vows with passion, "If I have done evil . . . let him trample my life to the ground."

Proverbs tells us that "pleasant words are a honeycomb, sweet to the soul and healing to the bones." Psalms takes it to heart: "Set a guard over my mouth, O Lord; keep watch over the door of my lips."

One might say that Psalms is the personal application of the advice in Proverbs. If Proverbs holds out a moral goal, Psalms is reaching out to seize it. And this is precisely the momentum, the "steadfast spirit," that we need in order to stop repeating the same old sins. We need to run toward a positive goal, not just avoid the familiar peril.

A habitually tardy boy, who slipped into his classroom late again, explained that the icy streets were so slippery that whenever he tried to move a step forward, he'd slide two steps back. The teacher thought this a sorry excuse. "If that were true," she asked, "how did you ever get to school?"

The boy replied brightly, "I finally turned around and went home!"

We progress in the Christian life, not by struggling against our slippery adversary, but by turning around toward where we really want to go. If in trying to eliminate some habit from your life you find yourself slipping backward, try facing the opposite direction: away from the sin and toward its antithesis.

We need something positive to aim at, not just something negative to avoid. Think of the kid who's just learning to ride a bike and is trying his best to go in a straight line. Often he'll glare resolutely at the bushes he's determined to avoid along the sidewalk—and end up wobbling right into them. Even though we may be trying to overcome a certain habit, we shouldn't primarily aim at it; we need to fix our gaze on exactly where we want to go—the more specific our goal, the better. We need a very clear picture of a certain moral quality in our mind that can draw us away from that glaring sin.

The usual candidates don't always stand up under pressure too well. Traits like self-control and purity typically line up as opposites for any number of habits. But these virtues can appear quite colorless compared to juicy tidbits of gossip or the fiery insistence of a bad temper or the gaudy pull of lust. In fact, self-control and purity as we usually picture them aren't so much counterpoint virtues as antisins. Self-control is not bursting out with this or that. Purity is not indulging in this or that. They don't stand alone as ends in themselves.

During my freshman year in college, I trudged up a long hill with a mixture of fear and expectation toward a small white house a few blocks from campus. It was a hot, quiet evening under a vast, moonless sky. Some students were having a prayer meeting there, which, I'd been told, was very unique. I'd heard these people in chapel describe their "discoveries" of the most ordinary things— like acceptance with God and salvation through Christ—with great excitement. I'd nodded off to such truths a thousand times, but they made everything sound totally new, like a revelation dropped from a divine satellite that was going to make all the difference in the world.

Feeling rather vulnerable, I entered the house and was met by wall-to-wall students sitting on the floor, all singing heartily. I sat down and listened to their lively tunes; these kids meant every word. I sensed an amiable spirit in the room, as if you could know others there immediately and deeply.

Then a junior religion major stood up and began drawing diagrams on a white board. He talked enthusiastically about how our sexual nature is related to the spirit, soul, and body concept in Scripture. The Bible shows us just how healthy relationships progress, he said. First, one establishes spiritual oneness with the other person. You grow together on that level. Then you progress through a mental and emotional give and take. And finally, when that bonding process leads to a commitment, you become one physically. Genuine oneness in the flesh is a climax of the intimacy that has preceded it.

The guy spoke as if the principles of the Bible were the last word on sexuality. I was entranced by this beautiful and coherent picture of what God intended human oneness to be.

All my life, growing up in Christian schools, I'd heard about sexual morality in terms of venereal disease and unwanted pregnancy. You waited until marriage in order to avoid certain calamities. It had never occurred to me that purity could be anything but slightly embarrassed defensiveness. But that night, God's positive image of sexuality won hands down over everything else.

That night proved to be a turning point in my life; I definitely warmed up to "things of the Spirit," which before had seemed remote and forbidding. And there I experienced for the first time the zeal of the psalmists in hot pursuit of virtue as if it were hidden treasure.

Chapter 8
How to Go Home Again

God makes a home for the lonely

Different things trigger it for different people. Air-conditioning and humid-hot days used to do it for me. Those sensations would send me back to Grandmother's house in Houston and to our reunions following my family's three-day drive up from Puebla, Mexico. We had no central air down there in the fifties, and the summers were rather dry. And so a certain cool smell from an air conditioner and a certain mugginess sometimes bring on a wave of nostalgia. I taste that childhood excitement of running into Grandmother's arms after the long Christmas trip and feeling the wonder of America again. And I feel homesick for a world that has disappeared.

Most of us catch a whiff of nostalgia on occasion that sends us back to that earliest home, some childhood Eden, and fills us with a longing for its warmth and security. A certain Levite, a son of Korah, had what we might call an industrial-strength case of homesickness when he penned Psalm 84. The temple, the center of his world, had been stripped bare of its gold and silver for tribute to a plundering Assyrian king named Sennacherib. The glory of the sacred place had been stolen.

And standing there, staring at this scarred shell, the Levite remembered how lovely the dwelling place of the Almighty had been and was overcome with nostalgia. He had known such wonderful times of communion with his Lord in that place.

> My soul yearns, even faints
>   for the courts of the Lord;

> my heart and my flesh cry out
>   for the living God.

But then the Levite spotted a sparrow nest near the broken stones of the altar and a swallow pecking in between the cracks for food for her young and realized that, even amid these signs of disrepair and disuse, this place was his home and his substance too.

> Blessed are those who dwell in your house;
>   they are ever praising you.

> Better is one day in your courts
>   than a thousand elsewhere.

What the Levite discovered is that you can go home again—in spite of what has happened to change things, in spite of physical decay. You can go home again if the Lord is what you're looking for. Worshiping God can be a great homecoming.

People need to know that they can go home again. Lonely people, cynical people, angry people, immoral people. We all need to know that the place where God meets us is still there.

The psalms as a whole furnish for us the home that is Yahweh. God Himself is home. They testify:

> Lord, you have been our dwelling place
>   throughout all generations.

The psalmists assure us that we are kept safe in the dwelling of God, hidden in "the shelter of your presence." God makes a home for the friendless. The psalmists promise that no harm will befall those who make the Most High their dwelling.

We can go home to God because He acts as a solicitous Father to us. In talking about the God who remembers our weakness and forgives, Psalm 103 states:

> As a father has compassion on his children,
>   so has the Lord compassion on those who fear him.

This "father to the fatherless" and "defender of widows" in the psalms is a foreshadowing of Jesus' unforgettable picture of the one running open-armed to meet his prodigal son. As David testified:

> Though my father and mother forsake me,
>   the Lord will receive me.

We can go home again. But often, as with the Levite of Psalm 84, we need a shock to the system in order to see what that home really is. We don't really recognize what we have until we lose it—or almost lose it.

Jerry and I walked into Room 311 at the worst time. Barbara, our stepmother, was trying to suction Dad, holding his restless tongue flat with a suppressor, wiggling the tube gingerly down his congested throat. "If only I could keep him suctioned for one day," she explained reflexively in greeting, "maybe the pneumonia . . ." and then paused to thank us for flying out from California. Her drawn face made it clear she'd been fighting a losing battle for some time.

I had come with anxious expectations. After the stroke, how pale and emaciated would his face be? I did not want to see those familiar ruddy features wasting away. But it wasn't his face, still holding a bit of color, that shocked. It was his terrible struggle for breath, chest and abdomen heaving, never a moment's rest. I wasn't ready for suffering.

Jerry had to leave to pick up our oldest brother Dan at the airport. After Barbara and I visited with the doctor, he left us with the suggestion that at some point the family might start thinking about when it would be appropriate to stop artificial-support systems. As we embraced in the hallway, I mumbled a few words to Barbara about heaven. It was the first time in my life I had referred to it as a present consideration.

At 3:00 p.m. the pastor and an elder arrived, old friends of the family. The pastor took out his tiny bottle of oil and rubbed a little on Dad's pallid, furrowed forehead. He placed a hand on Dad's numb shoulder and began to pray quietly. It was a very mild petition, just laying things out before the will of the Lord.

When Dan and Jerry arrived, there were polite hugs all around, clumsy words of encouragement for all present. My brothers said they would stay with Dad and urged me to go out for some food. I persuaded Barbara to take a break too.

Driving up the gravel road to Dad and Barbara's country house, I spotted the red barn he had built for his horses. While Barbara fixed a bite, I walked over to take a look.

Beneath a covering of leaves the grass looked terribly green, green as the tall stands I'd seen at Dad's boyhood farm near Texarkana. I stepped inside the barn and smelled the pungent hay. The horses were gone, but every beam stood sturdy as ever. Solid oak. He'd put up most of it by himself.

Dad built well. I remembered all the times I had relied on him. I remembered them well. I was five when I slipped off his back while he was climbing out of the swimming pool. I couldn't swim, but they say I just lay in the water calmly (sinking), sure that Dad would fetch me out again. And of course he did. I was twelve, walking with him in the woods he loved. It was always easy to talk. I had so many questions about right and wrong. And he lived the answers.

It was getting late. Shadows settled over the cornfields bordering Dad's place. I took a last look up at the sturdy oak rafters, breathed deeply the fragrance of wood and hay, and walked out into the dusk, grateful for good shelter.

Back at the hospital, Jerry and Dan reported that Dad had slept a while, breathing rather restfully for the first time. It was exhilarating news.

That night the three of us kept a vigil in Room 311, watching over the helpless man who once changed our diapers. He still heaved sometimes but was definitely sleeping more than struggling. On occasion he snoozed very quietly. His shallow but regular breathing sounded wonderful.

We didn't talk much, but our night watch felt good. We changed his position at regular intervals, fiddled with the blankets, and jumped up whenever he groaned.

Slowly I began to understand why Dad always got up around 2:00 a.m. to check on us and smooth our blankets—even after we were older. This was the only time I had been up in the night for the one who was up so many nights for me. This was unexplored territory. In its strange stillness I came face to face with the power of his love for me. I knew then that I will love my children with the same unquenchable desire.

About 10:00 Sunday morning, Dan, Jerry, and I returned to the hospital after a few hours of sleep. Nurses had disconnected the oxygen. Dad was breathing just fine on his own. They believed he'd licked the pneumonia. One said, "A miracle is just what we needed around here."

I walked over to the bed; Dad saw me and smiled. I grabbed on to the faint twinkle in his eyes for all I was worth. A good sign. Then he asked for water. I held a paper cup to his lips, he gulped, and swallowed, yes, swallowed, twice.

We spent the day congratulating Dad on his imminent recovery and exercising the languid limbs on his paralyzed right side. On Monday, it was time to fly back to our other families. Dad was making gains by the hour. We said goodbye in good spirits. At the airport the three of us reminded each other how fortunate it was we arrived right at the critical time. Our farewell embraces were strong and sure, no longer those of awkward, self-conscious children. We clutched at roots, almost torn up, that now bound us more visibly together within the miracle of a father's love. We had come home again.

God as our home is usually discovered from the inside. We are given a moment of recognition, and our hearts respond: Yes, that's the way God is. In my night watch at the hospital I was privileged to see a heavenly Father rescue the one who had showed me what He is like.

As high as the heavens

Fortunately, the Father we discover in the psalms doesn't have the usual male disabilities. He is not inept at sharing His emotions. We learn what fatherhood is all about by looking at Him. If you've thought that you have to wait until the New Testament to get a picture of boundless divine love, think again. Listen to the psalms. When we go home again, we discover what it means to be cherished.

Psalm 103 fairly bursts with the theme. The Lord who is compassionate and gracious, David sings, the One who forgives and heals, renews our strength like the eagle's. This God never treats us as our sins deserve. His love is pledged to us from everlasting to everlasting. His fatherly regard is qualitatively removed from what we human beings experience:

> As high as the heavens are above the earth,
> so great is his love for those who fear him.

Other psalms join in the celebration. God's love is present and active, the best news one could receive at the start of the day:

> Let the morning bring me word of your unfailing love.

God's love stands firm forever, faithful through all generations. The Lord is slow to anger and rich in love, loving toward all He has made. Psalm 136 falls into a chant about this divine regard, telling us twenty-six times that "his love endures forever."

All this can sound very sublime—but intangible. Those of us hassling with jobs, mortgages, teenagers, and noisy neighbors often wonder: Can this love really affect me where I am, with all my problems and insecurities and bad habits? Can it really fill the aching emptiness inside? We see this high-as-the-heavens love most clearly as it intercepts the least-promising lives.

Richard Wurmbrand began his adult life as a one-dimensional, zealous playboy in the Bucharest of the fifties, a place sleazy enough to be called "Little Paris." Doing well in business, he had plenty of money to spend on plenty of girls in flashy bars and cabarets. "I did not care what happened," Wurmbrand recalled, "as long as my appetite for fresh sensation was fed."

After his marriage he continued to chase women, breaking hearts, lying, asking of himself no questions about those he'd "seduced and slandered, mocked and bluffed."

But then Wurmbrand ran smack into a love as high as the heavens. In a hospital fighting off tuberculosis, this atheist read a Bible and was overwhelmed by the personality of Christ. He could not help comparing his own pathetically confined life with the nobility of Jesus. This encounter proved decisive. The life that slid along in a narrow rut of self-indulgence suddenly broadened. Wurmbrand decided to become a pastor.

Fast-forward several years to a Romanian prison, where Wurmbrand had been sentenced to a long term. There he failed both to be reeducated and to reveal any important Christian conspiracies against the government. And so he endured years of dreadful abuse and torture.

But in this hell Richard Wurmbrand survived as something of a Renaissance man, gifted in the art of deepening other people, all kinds of people. The pastor was able to relate to a whole menagerie of human beings passing through the dark of that prison.

There was Grecu, the dedicated Communist lieutenant, swinging his truncheon, demanding that Wurmbrand confess to a list of crimes. Given paper and pencil, Wurmbrand confessed faith in Christ, who bade him love his enemies. Grecu read the confession and began asking questions. Wurmbrand patiently and skillfully weaned the lieutenant away from ideology and into allegiance to a personal God.

Then there was Radu Mironovici, former leader of the Fascist Iron Guard, who claimed to be a Christian but constantly vented his hatred of Jews. Wurmbrand broke through his pride. He showed Radu that, according to his own orthodox beliefs, he was adding a few drops of Jewish blood to his Aryan blood every time he took communion.

Wurmbrand made prayer real for "the professor," a scholarly inmate who'd despaired of ever finding God. He managed to establish rapport with "Fingers," a calloused thief constantly talking of his exploits. The pastor found grounds for compassion even for the vilest offenders whom every prisoner despised. When fellow inmates abused a man who'd shot Jews by the hundreds, Wurmbrand interjected, "We don't know where he will spend eternity: If it's with Christ, we're abusing a future citizen of heaven; and if it's in hell, why add curses to his suffering?"

During seventeen years of suffering, Richard Wurmbrand ministered to human beings narrowed and distorted by a myriad of hatreds and prejudices. He kept finding ways to open hearts and broaden minds. He had a remarkable gift for identifying with the whole menagerie of sinners and saints, Fascists and Communists, clergymen and thieves, the broken and the proud. The one-dimensional playboy had met the Father of compassion. The love that is higher than the heavens had found a home in this very human heart.

Your face I will seek

The psalmists wax eloquent in the glow of divine love and do their best to make it real for us. But they do more. God's expressions of love inspire their own. These men respond to God with an ardor fired by the passion of the Father Himself. Nowhere else in the Bible do we find such profound expressions of personal devotion.

Psalm 42 pours out such a fervent language of love that we are almost tempted to avert our gaze.

> As the deer pants for streams of water,
>   so my soul pants for you, O God.

This man has found God as his home—in the very innermost part of his being.

> Deep calls to deep
>   in the roar of your waterfalls;
> all your waves and breakers
>   have swept over me.

The psalmist's words suggest that the awareness of God's love has been so intense at times that he can only compare it to a waterfall thundering through his heart.

Psalm 63 is another classic of devotion. It begins where most love poems leave off:

> O God, you are my God,
>   earnestly I seek you;
> my soul thirsts for you,
>   my body longs for you,
> in a dry and weary land
>   where there is no water.

This psalm testifies that our hearts can be satisfied with God as truly as our bodies "with the richest of foods." It even declares:

"Your love is better than life." David here attests a mind-boggling fact. If given a choice between experiencing God's love fully for a few minutes and living the usual seventy or so years, the former would be preferable.

These are men who indeed walk in the light of their Lord's countenance. They absorb a great deal of divine love because they have become participants in the language of divine love. Love grows as it is expressed. It doesn't flourish if left in some nice, quiet religious corner of our lives.

What the psalmists are laying before us is really a record of their devotional life: time spent with God in prayer and meditation on His Word. That's how we come home again; that's how God's love becomes real enough to fill us up—and fill all those holes that our background has left us with.

There's no substitute for meaningful time spent in communication with God. Without it, we're just staring at the outside of the temple (often stripped of gold and silver); we don't make it all the way home. With it, we discover that one day in the courts of God is better than a thousand elsewhere.

Too often, we approach the Word basically as a textbook full of doctrinal information. We tend to comb through passages, pulling out texts and phrases and words that support a certain position; we build up data to insert into the appropriate categories and fine-tune theories to fit them together. The more scholarly pore over Hebrew and Greek nuances and analyze grammatical structure. The less scholarly grab whatever proof texts come in handy and hang on for dear life.

The Bible does, as a matter of fact, have a lot of doctrinal information, and objectively analyzing and putting together its data is very important. But devotional study is something different; it goes beyond information. I happen to do a lot of analytical Bible study for various writing projects, and I do it regularly in the morning, but I've come to realize that it's possible to come away from all my neat categorizing and amassing of data with no more inspiration than from an hour of underlining a tome on biology. I need something more to make it devotional; I need to admire God.

Our primary purpose in looking at the Word is not to put theories or creeds together but to know a whole Person better. Trying to get all our doctrines to come together just right is worthwhile, but God can get lost in the shuffle; He can be fragmented into abstraction if we approach Him only through the many layers of our correct theology.

The psalmists never let us forget the bottom line:

> My heart says of you, "Seek his face!"
> Your face, Lord, I will seek.

One of the men whose devotion I admire the most is Charles-Eugène de Foucauld, the Trappist monk of the Sahara. However, Charles started out in life as a troublesome brat and got progressively worse. By the time he became an officer in the French hussars, he'd grown into a snobbish, licentious, gluttonous egotist—by his own account. But then he discovered something big enough to consume his vanity and overpower his voracious ego: Jesus Christ. Charles testified, "As soon as I believed there was a God, I knew I could not do otherwise than to live only for Him." Eventually he expressed his commitment by serving as a missionary to the nomad tribes of the Sahara and adopting their minimalist lifestyle.

In the middle of the desert, near a lonely French army post, he built a rustic chapel of palm beams. "Very poor," Charles admitted, "but harmonious and pretty." Four palm trunks held up the roof; a paraffin lamp threw light on the altar. On white calico he painted a large figure of Christ "stretching out His arms to embrace, to clasp, to call all men, and give Himself for all."

And there he cloistered himself, making out his island of devotion with a circle of pebbles. He rose in the dark early hours to pray and meditate, then received visitors, greeting them at the door dressed in the flowing robe of the desert people.

Charles also embarked on excursions out to desert settlements and encountered proud, veiled Tuareg warriors, as well as hungry nomads afflicted with ulcerated eyes, malaria, typhus, and gangrenous cuts. Slowly the Trappist earned their trust. They came to delight in this wiry holy man who spoke their language, required neither flattery nor gifts, and happily bestowed medicines, soap, flour, sugar, tea, and needles. One woman whose child Charles had saved from death, declared, "How terrible it is to think of a man so good, so charitable, going to hell because he is not a Muslim!"

He who had grown up amid aristocratic ease endured the harsh desert and even his harsher discipline with an easy cheerfulness because, when in prayer, he saw that his Lord was infinitely happy and lacked nothing—"Then I, too, am happy, and I lack nothing; Your happiness suffices me."

On rare occasions, when Charles found someone who could understand something of his feelings, he tried to share "the immense happiness which one enjoys at the thought that God is God and that He whom we love with our whole being is infinitely and eternally blessed." This is the theme one finds over and over in his letters. Charles is intensely happy that God is God. He feels "drowned in God." Here was someone rejoicing not just in God's blessings but in God Himself. He was not just devoted to a sublime feeling in the soul but to a separate greatness.

After Charles' death at the hands of rogue tribesmen, his life could be summed up in the few possessions discovered at his chapel: a breviary, a cross, a chalice, linen, and candlesticks. That is all. Here was an eloquent language in symbols, with each essential object laid out with passionate conviction.

Chapter 9
I Can Survive Anything

The heavens declare, the skies proclaim

It hit me all of a sudden one balmy Saturday afternoon by the pond near our house. I was in college and yet to hit on a legitimate career. Out for a walk around our pond and its ugly, unkept environs, I decided for some reason to sit down amid the tall grass and wait. And in the quiet I began to see.

Seven shades of green and gray. Textures. The skin of a beetle. A piece of bark. Nothing in that rather bleak episode of Illinois autumn shouted beauty. The colors were long gone. But everything around me did say "good"—with confidence. The dying scrub around me buzzed with what seemed like exotic insects. The scum on the pond's surface brought forth a wondrous array of insects. Every nondescript weed suddenly took on an intriguing character. I longed to know names and precise properties. What species did those long, slender leaves and those gray-brown fuzz balls belong to?

This was good, worthy of a human life's devotion. I had one of those primitive automatic cameras with me, the kind that cast a disinterested focus on the world in general. I peered through its tiny window and earnestly sized the contour of a stem, the flight of a dragonfly, not yet feeling ready to shoot a frame. I just waited. I felt honored to be silent and still, to do nothing but wait amid this miniature splendor in the grass and capture for the senses whatever might be given me.

And so my destiny was sealed. Someday I'd get a real camera. I'd become a nature photographer. I'd go deep into the warp and woof of creation and come out with glimpses of—God.

My destiny lasted about two-and-a-half weeks. Being a nature photographer had its weak points. But I did eventually get a decent camera, and photography did become a part of my work. And that sense of wonder did not entirely go away.

Early in my labors as a photographer I treated every snap of the shutter like a cosmic event—especially when aiming at nature. My poverty and the price of film had something to do with it. And I did not have sense enough to shoot up a great scene from every angle and f-stop.

Instead, I worked religiously for the one perfect shot. I remember in particular a series on flowers I did during my macro-lens phase. Extreme closeups held me fast at the time. Taking vengeance on that old automatic, I could now focus on a fly's navel.

Well, here was this flower, yellow petaled and perfectly symmetrical. How could I shoot it without making a cliché? I got close, of course. Into the pistil, around the pistil. Would this translucent gold ever reproduce on film? How about a side view, the curve of the petals? How about including the tip of another flower?

I worked an hour for a couple of pictures. They're nice. But looking back, I see that the reverence was what counted. Kneeling down and hovering over those splashes of yellow in the mud by my apartment, I still waited in earnest for glimpses. And those flowers, too, shouted "good."

In the psalms, the creation itself becomes a language that God articulates to us.

> The heavens declare the glory of God;
> the skies proclaim the work of his hands.

The elements don't just pose nicely for our benefit, they "pour forth speech"; their voice infiltrates every language and idiom on earth.

God makes "the dawn and the sunset shout for joy." When He comes to "judge the world in righteousness," the rivers clap their hands, and the mountains sing in chorus for joy. When the Almighty looks at the earth, it trembles; when He touches the mountains, they smoke. If the God of heaven and earth chooses to extricate Hebrew slaves from mighty Egypt, then nature enthusiastically cooperates:

> The sea looked and fled,
>   the Jordan turned back;
> the mountains skipped like rams,
>   the hills like lambs.

Clearly, nature is a language that God expresses and animates. He is not the captive of that language, tied up in its syntax. Rather, He can make it say what He wishes, when He wishes. Sometimes the Almighty makes it speak in ways that shock. In the wilderness He "turned the rock into a pool, the hard rock into springs of water."

One of our great privileges on this planet is to listen to that language as we look at the face of nature. And on occasion, the voice we hear becomes very distinct.

British chaplain Thomas Traherne saw "Eternity" in the broad daylight of an ordinary day when the green trees "transported and ravished me," and the dust and stones of the street seemed "precious as gold."

The poet e. e. cummings was once moved to psalm:

> i thank You God for most this amazing
> day: for the leaping greenly spirits of trees
> and for a blue true dream of sky; and for everything
> which is natural which is infinite which is yes

St. Francis of Assisi praised the God he felt come close in Brother Sun, Sister Moon, Brother Wind, Sister Water, and Mother Earth. He felt a kinship with God through all these. George Fox, founder of the Quakers, saw "creation . . . opened to me" and felt "wrapped up, as in rapture, in the Lord's power."

Fearfully and wonderfully made

Admittedly from a distance, nature can be reduced to Muzak, something pleasant in the background. From a distance we might even imagine that it's simply the result of time plus chance plus natural selection. But up close, this language exhibits a skill and a grammar that defy human powers of explanation.

It is evident that the psalmists have gotten up close. They stand in awe of God's power and skill. He releases elemental forces like memos:

He sends his command to the earth;
   his word runs swiftly
He spreads the snow like wool
   and scatters the frost like ashes.
He hurls down his hail like pebbles.
   Who can withstand his icy blast?
He sends his word and melts them;
   he stirs up his breezes, and the waters flow.

When David pondered his "unformed body" somehow "woven together in the depths" of the womb, he was moved to affirm:

I praise you because I am fearfully and wonderfully made;
   your works are wonderful,
I know that full well.

When the author of Psalm 147 looked up at the heavens one night and tried to take it all in, he was overcome by the magnitude of God's reach:

He determines the number of the stars
   and calls them each by name.

The choreographed stars of the universe sign down to us a strong suggestion of an infinite God who transcends all we can imagine. Nature up close appears to us as exhibit A of God's brand-name handiwork. It is a language that becomes compelling argument. Its mind-boggling complexity contends for a God with unlimited abilities.

Walking by a dandelion, we might only see a weed flapping in the breeze, but up close this plant becomes a prodigy of aviation. The common dandelion sends its seeds aloft by means of tiny parachutes. First, the plant actually measures relative humidity, temperature, and wind velocity. It will release its seeds only when conditions are just right. A steady wind must be blowing, not just a brief gust; the air must be warm and dry—indicating that rising wind currents will prevail. Only then do the flying seeds let go and venture on their all-important journey. And these dandelion seeds, hanging under their umbrellas like so many paratroopers, are able to travel remarkable distances.

Several other plants also transport seeds by means of parachutes. And what's very interesting is that these plants are from widely different botanical families. They are not confined to one species or genus; they are not one type of plant. This presents a real problem for the theory of evolution. It's one thing to assume that one plant group managed to evolve this ingenious parachute solution to the problem of seed transportation. That, in itself, takes a lot of faith. But to believe that a whole range of different plant types all developed this same amazing solution to a common challenge—takes more faith than I can muster.

From parachutes we move to gliders. The most interesting example is probably the winged seed of the tropical liana. It grows high up in the branches of its parent tree amid beautiful, shining green leaves. The liana seed develops two curved wings, transparent and gleaming, which are as elastic as sheet mica. When the seed releases from the tree, it glides away in the breeze.

Coldly objective scientists grow eloquent when observing this bit of plant aeronautics. One professor described the liana glider in this way: "Circling widely, and gracefully rocking to and fro, the seed sinks slowly, almost unwillingly, to the earth. It needs only a breath of wind to make it rival the butterflies in flight."

Early aviation pioneers were also impressed with the perfect flight of the liana seed. In building craft light enough to soar in the wind, stability was the key. Early flying machines kept falling apart. But the liana glider's gossamer wings were remarkably stable.

And so two flying pioneers, Etrich and Wels, made use of the liana seed in designing a tailless glider. The craft that resulted in 1904 proved to be a milestone in aviation history, gliding for about 900 meters. Another technological marvel that points to nature as the mother of invention.

Seeing things is something we take for granted, but up close, the eyes become an eloquent transcript of the Creator's ingenuity. The act of seeing is really an enormously complicated process. It begins when light strikes our eyes and is bent into focus at a precise angle by the transparent cornea. Next, the blue, brown, or green iris automatically varies the amount of light passing through by changing the size of the pupil.

After light passes through a colorless fluid called the aqueous humor (which is optically matched to the cornea and so keeps the rays bent at exactly the same angle), it reaches the tiny lens, made up of more than 2,000 infinitely fine layers of transparent fiber.

This lens, unlike the lens in a camera, is pliable. It can bulge slightly or flatten out. This changes the way light is bent and thus helps us focus very sharply.

Next, light travels (still on the same focused path) through a clear, jellylike substance that fills most of the interior of our eyes and reaches the retina, a pink coating that covers the back of the eyeball. The retina corresponds roughly to film in a camera. Packed into the retina lie what are called rods and cones. These photoreceptors contain light-sensitive pigments. About 130 million occupy an area the size of a postage stamp. Because of this, we are able to switch with relative ease from vision in bright sunlight to vision in a very dim room.

Our photoreceptors also transform light they receive into signals, partly electrical and partly chemical. Somehow, the light that created an image disappears, and in its place coded signals appear. To carry these signals, retinal fibers are required. These nerve fibers create a complex data-collection network that fans out over the retina. At a point in the back of the eye these fibers bunch together like a cable, becoming the optic nerve.

Now, things are just beginning to get complicated. The optic nerves from each eye crisscross in the brain. They exchange information in some way so that the images from two eyes can be coordinated into one stereoscopic field of vision. Then a new set of specialized nerve fibers pick up the signals and carry them to the visual cortex in the back of the brain. The actual phenomenon of "seeing" takes place in this small mass of gray matter.

The billions of cells in our visual cortex are arranged in a number of layers. All these cells have highly specialized functions. Some send projections to other areas of the brain where memory and association occur. Most add up, combine, exchange, and organize countless bits of visual data in some mysterious way yet to be fathomed. The result is the miracle of perception; a picture is produced in the mind through a process no high-tech computer can come close to duplicating.

This all leaves us with a big question: what came first? Did we develop rods and cones before the lens or vice versa? Did the optic nerve evolve first or the visual cortex? All the parts of this system function as an integrated whole. No single element would be of any use to an animal (trying to be the fittest to survive) without all the others. If we try to imagine that all the elements developed together in parallel fashion from simple to complex—all the while preserving 20-20 vision—then we do indeed believe in the wildest kind of miracle.

The language of nature ceaselessly presents its arguments before the court of reason, and human scientists haven't even begun to fathom all the evidence.

The desert overflows

The language of nature argues eloquently, but it can also give us great comfort. Going beyond polemics, it speaks in reassuring tones. And the psalmists heard that cadence. The Almighty, they saw, is not only powerful and skillful, He also provides and nurtures.

The author of Psalm 104 takes us on a tour of a world that overflows with the Creator's care. Springs pour down between the mountains to give water to the beasts of the fields. The earth yields its grasses and plants for our needs. Every creature finds a congenial home somewhere in the fruitful earth: the cattle in the grassy fields, the stork in pine trees, the wild goats in high mountains, badgers in the rocky crags. Birds of the air sing among the branches, the vast and spacious sea teems with creatures large and small, even lions prowling in the moonlit night "seek their food from God." The psalmist concludes: "When you open your hand, they are satisfied with good things."

In Psalm 65, David elaborates on the theme. When God visits the earth, it overflows. He softens the earth with showers, and our carts spill over with the year's bounty. The poet sees abundance everywhere:

> The grasslands of the desert overflow;
>   the hills are clothed with gladness.

The meadows are covered with flocks
  and the valleys are mantled with grain;
  they shout for joy and sing.

The psalmists absorbed a reassuring spectacle of God providing for us; they caught a glimpse of those lilies of the field and sparrows of the air that Jesus would elaborate on later. Nature up close tells us that God has resources to meet whatever needs we have.

We see that most clearly by visiting some of the worst places to live on earth. Take an area very few human beings have ever seen: the ocean floor. We know about as much about the surface of the moon as we do this forbidding region. But recently scientists in special research submarines designed to descend 8,000 feet or more have discovered tiny little creatures that simply shouldn't be there. The submarines went down to the edge of deep crevices and holes in the ocean bottom. Open vents there continually spew out superheated sea water under extremely high pressure. They are called "black smokers" and actually serve as chimneys, releasing heat from the earth's molten, unlivable interior. Temperatures at the vents have been recorded in excess of 570 degrees Fahrenheit.

At such heat, scientists have considered the existence of life as we know it inconceivable. Any creature would die instantly; its proteins and DNA would simply fall apart; its enzymes would melt away. Scientists who've studied Venus, for example, have ruled out the possibility of life on that planet because of its similar temperature.

But now two oceanographic scientists have discovered thriving colonies of what they've concluded are bacteria—living in water retrieved directly from these deep-sea vents. When these samples are sealed in pressurized chambers, brought to the surface, and heated to 480 degrees Fahrenheit, the organisms not only survive but also reproduce themselves. They can be killed only by cooling them down—in boiling water.

Under an electron microscope, these creatures look like ordinary bacteria, having the same basic structure. But amazingly enough they are able to live and thrive—in what amounts to a blazing, high-pressure inferno.

The God who clothes the valleys with grain has somehow given these bacteria the ability to adapt to and thrive in what appears to be a hostile environment. After all, the God of Scripture once enabled four faithful Hebrews to survive the fiery furnace of King Nebuchadnezzar. I find that very encouraging. Those bacteria tell me that God can help me survive anything. There's no fire so hot that He cannot help me adapt to it and, yes, even thrive in it.

This Creator has a variety of ways of helping us through the fire. Look at pine trees, for example.

Certain pine trees have even found a clever way to survive recurring forest fires. Adult pines are protected because of their thick bark and because their lofty crown of green needles reaches far above the flames. But how do they ever reach that height—intact?

Well, bright green pine seedlings grow fire-protecting outer scales, which, when burned away, leave the plants unharmed. The tiny seedlings may remain in this grass stage for six to twelve years, able to make it through one forest fire after another. But then suddenly, almost like a human adolescent, they experience one big growth spurt. The pines shoot up their now-vulnerable needles far above the flame zone.

From forest fires and "black smokers" at the bottom of the sea, let's travel to barren, frozen mountaintops in the Arctic. There, hardy explorers find incredibly tough plants, called lichens, growing in the cracks of porous rocks. In some places lichens can anchor themselves directly to bare rock, usually by digging into the surface with acids and then growing in the pits they've burned out.

Lichens can actually survive even when they remain frozen most of the year. They usually restrict their daily growing period to only an hour or two. So it can take a lichen twenty-five years to reach a diameter of one inch. But they can keep clinging to the inhospitable peaks for an incredibly long time. Old age for these hardy survivors may be 4,500 years.

The language of nature does offer comfort: with God's resources we can survive anything. The Creator who identifies Himself as the One who laid the foundations of the earth, who sends torrents of rain to a thirsty wasteland, who feeds the hungry lions, who brings forth the constellations in their seasons, who makes the eagle soar and the hawk take flight—this God will help us thrive in fire and ice.

Chapter 10
More in a World of Less

A thousand pieces of gold

It is a document that in our present world seems all but inconceivable: a poem about the law. Most of us can imagine breaking into rapturous lines about the man or woman of our dreams, about the beauties of nature, about the memories of a childhood home—but the law? Splash into purple prose about a series of religious precepts?

The law, for many people, is an impersonal entity imposed on us by impersonal institutions; our encounters with the law generally involve offended traffic cops, clogged courts, convoluted tax codes, zoning ordinances, or a maze of propositions on the ballot. Typically, we bump into the law as a barrier.

But in Psalm 119 we find an Israelite positively ecstatic as he contemplates the law of God. The psalmist rhapsodizes on the priceless heritage of God's precepts. With his lyre on the Judean hillsides, he makes the law musical. God's decrees, he tells us, "are the theme of my song." For this man, the law is more precious than a thousand pieces of gold, his heritage forever, a light on his path, trustworthy, true, a good counselor, sweeter than honey.

The author makes each verse in his stanzas begin with the same Hebrew letter—and each stanza features a succeeding letter in the Hebrew alphabet. The verses of stanza 1 all begin with *Aleph*, the verses of stanza 2 with *Beth*, and so on. In this way Psalm 119 suggests that the law encompasses all of life, just as the poem includes the whole alphabet. The author also uses a variety of words for *law* in each stanza, always employing at least six terms. He celebrates commands, statutes, precepts, laws, decrees, ordinances, word, and promise—like a musician poring over a masterful orchestra score, noting each nuance and shade of meaning.

How, we wonder, did this man find moral demands so stimulating? We are much more inclined to cringe than shout for joy on hearing them. What's his secret?

The first thing we need to understand about Psalm 119 is that the author saw the law as an expression of God's character. The law revealed God to him; it was very personal. In the Old Testament, "the word of God" and "the law of God" were often used interchangeably. So the law that is magnified in this psalm includes God's Word in general, His revelation of Himself in Scripture.

In the couplets of Psalm 119, the writer presented a series of parallel ideas. He equated remembering God's name with keeping His law. He juxtaposed the Lord's face shining down on His servant with being taught His decrees. He joined seeking Him wholeheartedly with not straying from His commands and God being near with His commands being true.

Those precepts and statutes the psalmist waxed eloquent over were not isolated entries in a thick code book; they were brush strokes that helped fill in the face of the Almighty, one more series of notes in the great score that expressed God's character.

Law is a black-and-white photograph of what God is like, or God in outline form. Scripture does not present God's law as some arbitrary code plopped down on the world but as something inevitable, ingrained in the universe.

The psalmist saw God's Word as eternal, standing firm in the heavens, suggesting the image of a sun shining down its blessings with clockwork regularity. He links God's faithfulness—that law which continues through all generations—with God's establishing the earth. He hints that God's decrees are as real as the form of our human bodies:

> Your hands made me and formed me;
>   give me understanding to learn your commands.

The law helped the psalmist know God and admire Him, so naturally he was eager to learn all he could. That's the first secret of Psalm 119. This man was admiring God; he enjoyed discovering more about Him: "Open my eyes that I may see wonderful things in your law." Of course he appreciated the law also as an invaluable guide in his life, but it was a personal guide, a personal word from the God who loved him.

Direct my footsteps

After we've discovered the law as an expression of God's character, we are left with an important question: Just how are we supposed to use it? Most of us have been able by now to make our way out of the Middle Ages and accept the fact that we can't be justified before God by "the works of the law." It is Christ's perfect obedience to the law's demands that, when accepted by faith, results in our redemption from the curse of the law.

But what about sanctification? What role does the law play in our growth? The familiar statement, "The law has been done away with," sometimes reflects the belief that we must live the Christian life by the promptings of the Spirit, not the letter of the law. Some sincere people even assert that the truly Spirit-filled believer no longer requires the guidance of the law at all. There are New Testament texts that talk about the futility of trying to progress in the Christian life by "the works of the law" alone. And Paul tells us that the new covenant is not of the letter of the law, which kills, but of the Spirit, which gives life.

New Testament writers make it clear that the law alone, without the Spirit, cannot help us. The law by itself often functions simply as a thermometer, measuring our moral temperature; it cannot make us well. So if we are trying to take on the law on our own, trying to obey it in our own strength, we will be frustrated.

But if the law without the Spirit is a dead end, so is the Spirit without the law. The new covenant involves the writing of the law on our hearts through the Spirit. We are given "the spirit of life" in Christ in order to fulfill "the righteous requirements of the law."

So, if the law without the Spirit is dead, then the Spirit without the law is mute. Law and Spirit are a dynamic process. We receive the Spirit through the Word, but the Spirit also helps us see more deeply into the Word. The two are mutually reinforcing. The Spirit is not just raw energy, contentless inspiration; it relates to factual information about God and results in insight. The Spirit keeps the law from becoming a dead letter because He helps us recognize God in the Word, not just dry precepts.

That's precisely the spirit that one catches in Psalm 119. Because the author is animated by God's presence, he finds the law of great help. It helps keep a young man pure. He finds that when his footsteps are directed by the Word, sin does not rule over him. He discovers that learning God's decrees prevents him from being consumed by his afflictions. When people slander him, he meditates on God's precepts and finds delight in them as in sympathetic counselors.

The psalmist enthusiastically recommends treasuring the Word in your heart and meditating on it in the night watches. He has found great peace and comfort in the Word, so much so that he can ask, "Be gracious to me through your law." Why? Because this isn't a list of impersonal requirements. It's the voice of the Spirit animating the language of God.

So back to our question. Has the law been done away with as a means of growth? Yes and no. It's true, we can't make progress by the law alone. But in the hands of the Spirit, God's law can become a living letter written on our hearts, moving us closer to Him.

We can see how the Spirit uses the law to great effect in the life of a young car thief in Santiago, Chile.

Samuel Espinoza had reached the top of the auto-theft business at the age of twenty. He'd managed to gather quite a following of criminals who admired his expertise. Samuel specialized in hot cars used in robberies as getaway vehicles. In one forty-five-day stretch his band of thieves stole sixty-seven automobiles.

But finally, on February 10, 1959, the long arm of the law caught up with Samuel. Apprehended and held for trial, he faced a long list of felony charges. Then, while awaiting trial, Samuel fell seriously ill with a paralyzing ailment. A Christian layman visited the young man in jail and told him about an influential friend he knew who could help. Samuel was interested. After several visits he discovered the man's "friend" was Jesus Christ.

Fortunately, Samuel remained interested. He learned to pray and began studying the Bible with enthusiasm. He began to place his faith in God. Doctors had told Samuel it would take from seven to ten years for him to recover, but within three months the paralysis had disappeared.

Finally, Samuel's case came to trial. He was hoping by some miracle he might be allowed to serve God on the outside, but on November 8, 1962, he was sentenced to twenty-five years in prison.

The youth spent a sleepless night pondering his future. He would be an old man of fifty when he got out. In the dark of his cell Samuel went through an agonizing time of introspection. He relived all the excitement and danger that had filled his life till then—but this time from a very different perspective. Samuel no longer felt like the cocky leader of a dangerous gang. The evil he'd done was tearing him apart. This young man was feeling the righteous weight of the law pressing down on him; he felt convicted before God.

But fortunately Samuel didn't get stuck there; he permitted the law to lead him to Christ. Alone in his cell, he spent a long time praying, seeking the God who seemed far away from his Santiago jail. And God reached out to this repentant youth. Samuel experienced a profound sense of forgiveness and acceptance by the Lord. He felt the past had been taken care of. In those hours he experienced the beginning of a rebirth through the Spirit.

The next morning Samuel felt like a new man. The guards were amazed at the cheerfulness of this prisoner facing a twenty-five-year sentence. Friends visiting him were happily surprised to see a look of peace on his face. Samuel said he was ready to serve God—anywhere, under any conditions.

That evening at nine he received a summons for questioning. It seemed an odd time for an interrogation. Why more inquiries the day after his sentencing?

Samuel spent an hour waiting in the warden's office and answering a few questions that seemed quite irrelevant to his case. Then he was told to gather his meager belongings. He was free to leave.

A stunned Samuel stepped through the main gate of the penitentiary and out into a pouring rain. He walked down the street in a daze, letting the water pelt him, breathing free air. Suddenly his sordid past was gone, washed away. The countless robberies blotted out, just like that. God's hand of mercy seemed graphically evident.

Needless to say, after his inexplicable release, Samuel felt wonderfully free in the Spirit. But he used that freedom well. His life began to reflect a righteous God so well that other people were won to faith because of his witness, including a youth behind bars.

Set in a wide place

In a recent *Time* essay, Charles Krauthammer talked of how unserious about moral distinction we've become. There's a moral AIDS running loose, he maintained, an acquired immune deficiency syndrome of the spirit. He wrote of "moral exhaustion, an abdication of the responsibility to distinguish between shades of gray. The usual excuse is that the light has grown pale; the real problem is a glaze in the eye of the beholder."

We are living in a world of less. And religious people, I believe, are finding themselves living with less and less too. I hear it among very earnest people who say, "Jesus is the only thing that counts. Nothing else matters; there are no rules."

Most of us know about the dangers of legalism. Its symptoms stand out like a sore thumb: an obsessive concern with petty dos and don'ts, endless attempts to be more strict than one's neighbor. But have we ever considered that we can be legalistic in a different way, that is, by always looking for the minimum, always trying to do just enough to get by?

Caring too much about the wrong things is a problem. But not caring about much of anything is a danger too.

Are we carving our religion down to the minimum in this world of less and less? Are the choices that we make all headed in one basic direction?

We don't want to be "too strict" about Sabbath observance. Some of the old taboos just don't make sense. Fine, but do we create new ways to celebrate the Sabbath meaningfully to replace the old? Is it still a special day that stands out in the week? Or do we just settle for less?

We don't think we should be forced to give money only through prescribed church channels. We want to be more spontaneous. OK, but do we find new ways to be generous? Or do we just give less?

We grow tired of the same old worship routine, the same old devotional readings with our family that everyone yawns through. This shouldn't be just a dull duty. Fine, but do we look for new ways to make family devotionals interesting, new ways to share and interact? Or do daily worships just trickle away altogether? We settle for less.

Less is not the solution to legalism. It just substitutes an enervated religion of the minimum for an exhausting religion of the petty maximum.

The solution is suggested by that poet waxing eloquent under clear Judean skies. In his mind, the law was essentially expansive, not restrictive. Listen to him exult:

> I run in the path of your commands,
> for you have set my heart free.

These are not the words of someone trying to toe the line but of a man freely expressing newfound abilities. In the law there is room to run; he didn't feel confined at all:

> I will walk about in freedom,
> for I have sought out your precepts.

The Hebrew word translated *freedom* can literally be rendered "a wide space." Seeking out God's precepts doesn't shove us into the closet of the strait-laced; it opens a passage to the great outdoors, a wide space where the good life begins.

This psalmist sensed in the law the promise of a life without oppressive boundaries:

> To all perfection I see a limit;
> but your commands are boundless.

He did not try to obey just out of a sense of obligation—putting square pegs into square holes—but because "your statutes are wonderful."

The author of Psalm 119 wanted more in a world of less. He wanted to experience the richness of life with God, and the law helped him along in that direction. It was bound up with God's animated Spirit as, seven times a day, he praised God for His righteous laws and lifted up his hands to the Lord's commands.

Either we can view God's standards as restrictive and try to do just enough to get by, or we can view them as doors opening the way to God's wide spaces. They take us to a place of abundance; they urge us to experience more of the truly good life. And when we follow that lead, energized by the Spirit, we will discover that the Word can widen us even in the most stifling of places.

In 1939, a young German theologian on a lecture tour in America was urged by his friends to take up some safe work in the States and not return to the deteriorating situation in his homeland. But he couldn't. Dietrich Bonhoeffer decided to take a stand with fellow believers about to be engulfed in the madness of Nazism. He departed on one of the last ships to leave for Germany.

Soon afterward, Bonhoeffer became a leader of the "Confessing Church," which resisted the philosophy of the brown-shirted fanatics. Because of his participation in a plot against Hitler, Bonhoeffer was captured, imprisoned, and sentenced to be hanged. Now this brilliant young man's world had shrunk dramatically. His bright future had collapsed into the small cubicle of his cell. One of that cell's previous inmates had scratched a bitter message on the floor. It read: "In 100 years it will all be over."

And yet Bonhoeffer found an alternative to despair, an alternative to a world of less and less. In the letters he wrote from prison before his execution, one senses a man who could expand—even in the shadow of the gallows. He wrote: "I am reading the Bible straight through from cover to cover, and have just got as far as Job, which I am particularly fond of. I read the Psalms every day, as I have done for years; I know them and love them more than any other book."

Many of his letters reflect on the meaning of Bible passages he'd been studying. Scripture was more than just a source of theology for Bonhoeffer; it remained his very personal companion and comfort. He described one terrifying day in this way: "The heavy air raids, especially the last one, when the windows of the sick-bay were blown out by the land mine . . . and I lay on the floor in the darkness with little hope of coming through the attack safely, led me back quite simply to prayer and the Bible."

Because Bonhoeffer remained open and responsive to the Word of God, his spirit blossomed in the confines of that prison. As a result he had a remarkable impact on all who met him. An English officer imprisoned with the theologian during his last weeks remembered him this way: "Bonhoeffer . . . was all humility and sweetness; he always seemed to me to diffuse an atmosphere of happiness, of joy in every smallest event in life, and of deep gratitude for the mere fact that he was alive. . . . He was one of the very few men that I have ever met to whom God was real and close."

Chapter 11
Recovering a Sense of Wonder

Marvelous deeds and mighty works

Years ago, the Coca-Cola Company conducted one of the most successful advertising campaigns in history. "Drink Coca-Cola" placards became almost as ubiquitous as street signs. That distinct logo with its handwritten type style in red and white was plastered everywhere—on billboards and bus-stop benches, in magazines and newspapers. Coke became America's number one–selling soft drink.

But then something happened. All those nice sales graphs started leveling out. The company wasn't making much progress anymore. And after much study, they started taking all those signs down. What researchers had discovered was that the once-distinctive "Drink Coca-Cola" logo had become invisible. The signs were so familiar they'd become part of the landscape; they didn't register.

We face a similar problem in the Christian life. Christian slogans that once elicited our hearty amens just slide through our minds after a while without making any ripples. This is especially true for those of us who have grown up in the church. We've heard it all before. Yes, God loves me. Yes, Jesus saves. We nod our drowsy assent, but the language doesn't really register anymore. It's so familiar that the words are all but inaudible.

I recall driving through midtown traffic one day, listening to a sermon on cassette someone had lent me. The minister introduced his subject by saying, "If I had announced my topic as 'Satanism

Today,' this auditorium would probably be packed. But I am speaking this morning about the love of God. And so you see these empty seats." He lamented the fact that people were more interested in demonism than in agape love.

I was sort of lamenting that fact, too, and wondering why we're that way. But then the speaker himself gave me a clue. He proceeded to give a very neat, orderly exposition of the components of divine love: A, B, and C, getting it all down with the right abstractions. If he had been talking about "Satanism Today," I realized, we would have heard stories of tables rattling, the deceased reappearing, and victims writhing on the floor. And we would have reacted with a sense of wonder because the supernatural world had become very real to us during those moments.

What those of us nodding off to the same old story need most is to see God active and present before us. People often talk wistfully about recovering their "first love" with the Lord; we also need to recover a sense of wonder.

And that's what the psalmists give us. They speak with the language of wonder. God has not yet become for them some benign blob in the sky. They speak in exclamations because they come fresh from the moral equivalent of tables rattling and people writhing on the floor. They bear witness to Yahweh's mighty works. And so He becomes a vivid, larger-than-life protagonist in their verse.

The psalmists are full of wonder, first of all, because God is sovereign over all. He rules the surging sea and scatters enemies. He sits enthroned between cherubim, exalted over all nations. When He sends commands to the earth, "his word runs swiftly." His summons flash "from the rising of the sun to the place where it sets."

When the Hebrews grow conceited in their temple, God reminds them that He doesn't need their sacrifices; after all, every animal in the forest, every bird in the mountains, and the cattle on a thousand hills are His. "If I were hungry I would not tell you."

El Shaddai rides the ancient skies above and thunders with a mighty voice, majestic over Israel. The Mighty One, the King above all gods, holds the depths of the earth in the palm of His hand.

This is no absentee executive, but a God of marvelous deeds and mighty works whom the psalmists look upon with awe. We can catch some of their sense of wonder by looking at an example of the

Sovereign in action. He displays His authority most clearly when He is discrediting adversaries and winning our ultimate allegiance.

Early in his career in the 1920s, the great Chinese writer and preacher Watchman Nee spent a New Year's holiday with five other young believers, trying to evangelize the village of Mei-hwa. The men had difficulty getting a hearing amid all the noisy celebrations. By the ninth day, the farmers and fishermen still weren't listening. One of the frustrated evangelists asked, "What's wrong? Why won't you believe?"

He was informed that Mei-hwa already had a reliable deity, Ta-Wang. The day of his festival, made known by divination, was fixed for January 11. For the past 286 years, the villagers affirmed, Ta-Wang had provided unfailing sunshine for the day he chose.

The headstrong evangelist exclaimed, "Then I promise you, our God—who is the true God—will make it rain on the eleventh." His hearers seized the challenge. If Jesus could make it rain on the eleventh, they would certainly listen to Him.

Watchman and the others with him were at first horrified by their brother's declaration. Was their God being presumptuously put on the spot? But after the men prayed very earnestly over the matter, a phrase from Scripture flashed into Watchman's mind: "Where is the God of Elijah?" Watchman felt assured that rain would fall on the eleventh. So the evangelists spread the challenge widely.

That evening their host informed them that half the villagers were fishermen who spent months out at sea and could be relied on to forecast the weather accurately for days ahead. The odds for rain on the eleventh seemed bad indeed. But again Watchman was assured by the words, "Where is the God of Elijah?"

On the morning of the eleventh, the evangelists were awakened by brilliant sunlight shining through their window. Quietly they gathered for breakfast. No sign of a cloud in the sky. As they bowed to say grace, Watchman observed, "I think the time is up. Rain must come now. We can bring it to the Lord's remembrance." They did so.

The first drops of rain hit the roof tiles before their Amen. As the men ate their rice, the drizzle became a steady shower. On being served a second bowl, Watchman paused to give thanks and ask for even heavier rain. It began coming down by the bucketful. At the end of breakfast, the street outside was deep in water.

A few faithful Ta-Wang supporters had carried their idol in a sedan chair outside, hoping his presence would stop the shower. But once they reached the street, the steady rain became a downpour. After a few yards the bearers stumbled in the flood. Ta-Wang fell and fractured his jaw and left arm.

Still they would not acknowledge defeat. The faithful repaired Ta-Wang and made fresh divination. A mistake had been made. The festival was supposed to be on the fourteenth.

Watchman and his men retired to pray. They asked for three sunny days and rain at 6:00 p.m. on the fourteenth, when Ta-Wang's procession would begin.

For the next few days the evangelists preached to large audiences under blue skies. The fourteenth began as another perfect day. When evening approached, Watchman and his friends brought their request to God and, not a minute late, His answer came with torrential rains and floods.

Even there your hand will guide me

Before we follow, before we imitate, before we do anything in the Christian life, we are asked to do just one thing: admire God. That's where a healthy process of growth begins, and it's a crucial step that's sometimes overlooked. We are typically urged to get on to the list of right behavior or on to assimilating the list of right doctrine. But the new birth begins, and each day in our Christian life should begin, simply with our looking up in awe.

People who try to follow God's will without coming to admire Him, and, yes, like Him, will soon burn out. You can't sustain imitation simply on the basis of duty or obligation. Imitation comes naturally only to those who are inspired. And we have to take time to look in order to be inspired.

The psalmists took time to look. And the wonderful thing is that they kept seeing more and more of God to admire. He proved to be an inexhaustible source of inspiration. "His greatness no one can fathom," they exclaim. "His understanding has no limit."

The author of Psalm 89 asks:

Who in the skies above can compare with the Lord?
Who is like the Lord among the heavenly beings?

And the author answers with the language of wonder: The Lord is "more awesome than all who surround him."

Part of the wonder of this limitless God is that He is present everywhere, knowing everything. The psalmists did not approach this as a theological category that required dissection; they approached it with the whites of their eyes showing. Here's the classic expression of wonder on the subject from Psalm 139:

> If I go up to the heavens, you are there;
>   if I make my bed in the depths, you are there.
> If I rise on the wings of the dawn,
>   if I settle on the far side of the sea,
> even there your hand will guide me,
>   your right hand will hold me fast.
>
> Even the darkness will not be dark to you;
>   the night will shine like the day,
> for darkness is as light to you.

David here sees in the divine omnipresence, not a divine essence sprayed everywhere, but a Companion always there for him, Someone who brightens every nook and cranny of life. And because he sees the vastness of the Almighty in terms of His omnipresent actions, he joins in the language of wonder:

> Such knowledge is too wonderful for me,
>   too lofty for me to attain.

One day in 1961, a Christian believer in Siberia had a most unusual dream. He was told to go to Moscow, where he would find a Bible for the church he attended. The man resisted the idea at first, knowing that Moscow's churches had precious few Bibles of their own. But the dream had seemed so vivid and authoritative. And he kept thinking of his 150 fellow church members without a single copy of Scripture among them. So the man set out on a journey 2,000 miles across the tundra.

About that time, another believer, the same Brother Andrew, and his companion Hans drove their VW from Holland down

through Germany and Poland, crossed the border into Russia at
Brest, and traveled on 700 miles to Moscow. Soon after arriving in
the city, the two men decided to check out the midweek service at
a certain Baptist church. They hoped to make contacts there so
they could unload some hot merchandise. Andrew and Hans had
managed to maneuver past border checkpoints and prying guards
with a load of Russian Bibles tucked away in their car.

But distributing the Bibles was as risky as slipping them
through the Iron Curtain. You never knew who might be a KGB
informant in a church or even if the pastor was under pressure to
report everything.

So when Andrew and Hans walked into the Thursday-night
meeting carrying a sample Russian Bible, they had a plan. After
the service the two lingered, checking out the 1,200 worshipers
milling past. Each man prayed that God would direct him to
someone he could safely entrust with his smuggled Scriptures.

Soon Andrew spotted a thin, balding man in his forties standing
against the wall. He felt a familiar "moment of recognition." The
directive to talk to the man seemed very clear, but Andrew waited
for Hans. Before Andrew could speak, his companion said, "I've
spotted our man!" In that vestibule crowded with hundreds of
people, Hans nodded toward the worshiper Andrew had chosen.

With hearts thumping they walked up to the stranger and
attempted to introduce themselves and explain where they'd come
from. He only stared at them, perplexed, until he caught the word
Dutch. It turned out he spoke German. So the three began a
vigorous conversation in that language.

Andrew and Hans listened incredulously as the man told his
story. This was the believer who'd come all the way from Siberia to
find a Bible for his church, hoping against hope that God would
somehow come through on the dream. Hans had the privilege of
delivering the good news: "You were told to come westward for
2,000 miles to get a Bible, and we were told to go eastward 2,000
miles carrying Bibles to churches in Russia. And here we are
tonight, recognizing each other the instant we meet."

When Hans handed the Siberian the Russian Bible they'd
brought, he was speechless. He stared at the book, then at the two
Westerners, then back at the book. Finally it all sank in, and he

burst out with a stream of thank-yous and bearhugs. Andrew managed to calm him and whispered that there were more Bibles; he could have a dozen to take back home the next morning.

God's reach stretches from horizon to horizon, and yet His presence never thins. He is all there in the dreams of a Siberian Christian, and at the same time He's traveling with Andrew and Hans as they navigate toward their incredible rendezvous.

The blazing fire

The psalmists' sense of wonder extended to one divine quality that many of us might find rather forbidding: God's unapproachable holiness. These men do not shy away from the subject; they pour on it their fresh admiration.

The author of Psalm 99 celebrates this divine quality in the phrase he repeats after each chorus. Why do we praise that "great and awesome name"? Because "he is holy." Why do we exalt the Lord and "worship at his footstool"? Because "he is holy." Why do we worship God "at his holy mountain"? Because "the Lord our God is holy."

The psalmists are convinced:

> The Lord is righteous in all his ways
> and loving toward all he has made.

They take great comfort in the fact that:

> The Lord is gracious and righteous;
> our God is full of compassion.

"Enthroned as the Holy One," "arrayed in holy majesty," He remembers "his holy promise" and extends "his holy arm" to work salvation, blessing with His "Holy Spirit." And so those who "worship at his holy mountain" and "bow down toward [His] holy temple" praise and glory in "his holy name," declaring: "Your ways, O God, are holy."

This God isn't just good, He shines forth "perfect in beauty." He is radioactive in holiness: "A fire devours before him, and around him a tempest rages."

The psalmists did not feel at all threatened by this divine character. They freely admired Someone whose righteousness was qualitatively far removed from their own. We catch an admiring glimpse of this holy fire best when we see it ignite those least likely to be concerned about righteousness.

For those awakened from a spectacularly sinful life, God's holiness sets off an obvious conflagration. Alcoholics become nurturing fathers; drug pushers turn into conscientious elders of the church. The flames throw evil into stark outline. Divine ideals glow in contrast. He strikes a spark not only for the flagrant sinner but for the decent citizen as well.

In the conservative, religious world in which I grew up, the greatest sins on the horizon were things like yelling at your brother, goofing off in church, or sneaking off with an extra piece of chocolate cake. I had no big red-lettered sins to repent of. I never had the opportunity to suddenly stop shooting dope or stealing because I never got started.

But looking back, I see God's justice has been very much alive and well in my life. I've felt the heat.

In the third grade, Pepe and I thought Juanita was pretty hot stuff. We expressed our admiration by tormenting the poor girl. One day during a break in class, Juanita teased us back. She shook her curls haughtily and gave us a big shove. I pushed her, too, right into the big wastebasket in the corner of the room. She fell back and smacked her head against the wall.

The teacher ran over. There was a little blood. They rushed Juanita over to the infirmary, where a couple of stitches were required. I felt like I'd just taken human life.

As I walked slowly home, all of creation pointed accusingly at me, the murderer. My parents were angry, of course. But the evil itself loomed larger. I had hurt another human being, and that burden seemed more than I could bear.

Adela, our housekeeper, fixed my favorite enchiladas that night. Everything tasted awful. Poking morosely at the food, I wondered, "How can I ever atone for what I've done? How can I ever erase the sound of that crack against the wall?"

We smile later about how innocent and naive we were as children, about how we exaggerated those minor transgressions. But maybe kids aren't so naive as we mature adults assume. Maybe they see more, not less. Fresher from being created in God's image, not yet dulled by a thousand moral compromises, they know. More truly than their elders, I sometimes think, children know the fire. At any rate, God's justice accompanied me through the years. It stood watch around me and then seeped inside. I was reading His Word, praying, believing Him. I remember stopping and looking back. How self-centered I'd been a few years before. I saw selfish decisions so clearly. I knew God's justice had awakened me further.

That kept happening. God's righteousness always stretched out ahead of me and drew me along in its wake. I never ran out of it. Almost all kids at some point reach the end of their parents' store of conscientiousness. I'm thankful that my parents were very consistent, but most kids approaching the teen years run into some little compromise, some collapse between the should and the will.

The shock hits hard. Kids feel suddenly bare against the world. They scramble for something to hang on to. The "rebel without a cause" begs his father to stand for something.

But my heavenly Father did stand—for uncompromising righteousness. I always found more of it to admire, more of it to seek. It never stopped. As I matured, His goodness deepened and broadened ahead of me. The righteous Lord wasn't just infinitely good in a child's eyes. During my college days God still led the way. I remember how hard certain verses about purity hit me when I was struggling with lust—after spring break on a campus full of comely coeds taking in the sun. You struggle for something resembling a clean mind so that every single female passing by doesn't become a piece of meat to "check out."

You check out, instead, a few verses of Scripture, and the sparks fly. You read in the book by Job, of all people, a vow: "If my step has turned from the way, or my heart followed my eyes . . . let my crops be uprooted." Instantly you see your sleazy heart following your bulging eyes. The vow sinks home.

Into adulthood I still felt the heat—and was warmed by it. That divine holiness was, for me, an enormous room in which I could grow freely. His goodness created a space for me to be. His righteousness had carved out lovely furniture. I could rest, admiring, in His accomplishments—and absorb them. I could put my hands out toward the huge fire blazing in the corner. It would never go out.

Chapter 12
Joy of the Burden Bearer

At my right hand

After the psalmists had craned their necks up at the heavens and marveled at this God who choreographs the movements of galaxies and causes mountain ranges to tremble at His touch, after they'd beheld the all-powerful God who is sovereign everywhere, they saw something rather different nearby. This same CEO of the universe could also act as the close companion of individuals. The Almighty wasn't just a generalized deity spread about everywhere or a remote ruler pointing His long scepter down to earth; He could be right here, right now.

David assures us in Psalm 145:

> The Lord is near to all who call on him,
> to all who call on him in truth.

The psalmist typically finds a deep sense of well-being in the fact that God is right next to him:

> Because he is at my right hand,
> I will not be shaken.

This closeness is possible, not just on some sacred mountaintop, but in daily life as well. Mortals may not only "gaze upon the beauty of the Lord" in His temple but also "walk in the light of [His] presence." The Hebrew poets discover that He is not just there in times of religious rapture but also "a very present help in trouble."

106

Himeji, Japan, 1976

Haruo leans forward, pressing his point home. "You wonder how I can believe in all this intangible religious stuff? Well, what if I told you there are private detectives and samurai battles, Hawaii beaches and lovers' dialogues, floating around in our room right now? You would find that hard to believe too, wouldn't you?"

Seigi nods.

Haruo reaches over and turns on the television. "But it's true. I can't sense the dots of color that float into this TV set, but I can tell by the results I see that something invisible is acting on the television.

"It's the same with God. He can be known by His actions. At first, I found the talk about angels and God's Spirit living in people pretty odd too. But I've seen the results in people's lives."

"Cut. That was great!"

Haruo and Seigi were doing a good job of acting out the parts of a new Christian and his skeptical friend. They had become accustomed to the heat of 2,500-watt lights and the purring of my Super-8 camera. Kazko, the Bible teacher who translated my script, was coaching the two young men well.

The film was my attempt to show that God is active and knowable. I was also hoping it would help solidify the faith of Haruo and Seigi, both new believers.

This was to be our last night of filming. The camera had to be back in another city the following day, so we were trying to squeeze in the final retakes.

One of Seigi's lines hadn't been recorded properly the previous week. We set up to shoot him in a close-up. He sits behind a low table looking over the script. The lights are adjusted to lose his shadow on the wall. Camera and mike are ready. We roll. Seigi does his isolated line pretty naturally, but the camera sputters and skips. Groan. I check all the wires, battery light, batteries, switch, and lock. Everything seems OK. I shake the film cartridge.

Lights. Second take. Seigi is into his line, but the camera still rattles unevenly. Please not now. Just a few little pickup shots and the film will be done. Disgusted and desperate, I take out the old batteries, which are working fine, and insert a new set into the camera grip.

Lights. Take three. The camera stutters again. "OK," I tell Seigi, "let me roll about ten feet of film in case something is jammed in the cartridge." For some reason I put the old batteries back in.

Lights again, please. Take four. I squeeze the switch with great intensity and shoot a minute of film, willing it to clear. No go. The camera sputters on, doggedly erratic.

My head goes hot and blank. I stare at my little black blankety-blank camera, completely flustered. There are no more switches or cables to fiddle with.

Then Kazko makes a suggestion, "Let's pray about it."

So the four of us kneel together, tell the Lord about our genuine need, and put our trust in His abilities.

We finish praying and look at each other for a minute. I stare at the recalcitrant camera. There's nothing more anyone can do.

Take five. Action. The camera makes such a melodious purr in my ear that I can hardly hear Seigi's line. The chronic sputtering is gone. We're all shouting together, slapping each other on the back.

We shot without a hitch the rest of the evening and completed the film. I was anxious to see our last roll. As soon as the footage came back from the lab, I projected Seigi's one-line pickup. The picture frame jumped and skipped during the first four takes; the sound wandered out of synch. On the fifth take, picture and sound were perfect.

I rushed off to tell Haruo, Seigi, and Kazko. We celebrated a completed project and also our glimpses of immanence. Haruo and Seigi had heard plenty about the God of heaven. But they said they'd never experienced Him brush by so close. He seemed to be projected up there, waving at us on the fifth take. God in a close-up, with His hands dirty, fiddling with camera parts.

He delights in me

Because the psalmists saw this God of heaven and earth as a close Companion, their language of wonder often turned into a language of joy. As David exclaimed, "In thy presence is fulness of joy."

These men came to the conclusion that God is very present with us, not merely out of obligation, but because He actually enjoys it. God Almighty likes to hang around human beings. I don't think any deity in the ancient world was ever pictured in quite this light. Listen to these unassuming, spontaneous expressions that conceal a revolutionary theological idea.

> The Lord takes delight in his people,
>> he crowns the humble with salvation.
> Let the saints rejoice in this honor
>> and sing for joy on their beds.

The author of Psalm 147 echoed:

> The Lord delights in those who fear him,
>> who put their hope in his unfailing love.

The clear implication is that Yahweh delights to have relationships with us based on respect and trust. That's what brings Him joy. David enlarged on the theme: "The Lord . . . delights in the well-being of his servant." "He rescued me because he delighted in me."

God's joy in being present with us proves contagious; we are moved to rejoice in this honor and sing for joy at the thought. The psalmists compose songs "to God, my joy and my delight." They bring "whole burnt offerings to delight you," take delight in His salvation, even delight in His laws to no end. Their most earnest admonitions are often framed in the language of joy:

> Delight yourself in the Lord
>> and he will give you the desires of your heart.

Men and women down through history have joined their testimony to that of the psalmists: God does delight in coming close.

The peasant saint Brother Lawrence discovered that "we may make an oratory of our heart, wherein to retire from time to time, to converse with Him in meekness, humility, and love."

The mystical writer Lady Julian of Norwich felt that "God is closer to us than our own soul."

Dwight L. Moody in his early days as an evangelist wanted God that close. He was praying earnestly for God's Spirit to fill him. And He did. It happened one day while he was walking down a street in New York City. God arrived altogether. His love overwhelmed Moody. The experience was so intense, he recalled, that "I had to ask Him to stay His hand." The man couldn't contain all that was poured into him.

Singer Ethel Waters as a teenager knelt at the "mourner's bench" during the last night of revival meetings in her town and prayed hard. She felt a great need of something in that little church and yet didn't know exactly what it was. So she asked: "What am I seeking here? What do I want of You? Help me!"

Then she found "the peace I had been seeking all my life. Love flooded my heart and I knew I had found God and that now and for always I would have an ally, a friend close by to strengthen me and cheer me on." Church members told Ethel afterward that she appeared as one transfixed and that the light in her face electrified the whole church.

The psalmists knew, of course, that God doesn't dwell inside us in the most literal sense. He doesn't constrict His existence to the inner life of human beings. But the remarkable fact is this: He is there altogether, as if we alone shared His intimate companionship, as if we alone received the full force of His divinity within. The measure of His unique closeness is that He makes individuals feel that way. As David declared in Psalm 139:

> How precious to me are your thoughts, O God!
> How vast is the sum of them!

The Ruler of the universe is thinking about me! And He takes delight in our relationship. There are no boundaries, no dark pockets, no reservations in God's heart. His delight reverberates pure and unrestrained. This joy of the Most High enables people to transcend their surroundings, sometimes in remarkable ways.

Malcolm Muggeridge, British journalist, watched as his dream of a socialist kingdom of heaven on earth dissolved before his eyes. Gray, starving figures aimlessly padded the gray streets of Russia's cities at the height of the collectivization famine in the 1930s. True believers in socialism still sent out press releases describing bursting granaries and rosy-cheeked dairymaids in the Ukraine. But Muggeridge could no longer speak.

So he went to listen, instead, at an Easter service in Kiev's Orthodox church. The place was packed. Standing in the congregation that slowly wedged its way toward the altar, Muggeridge felt himself pressed against a stone pillar, scarcely able to move.

But that's not what took his breath away.

He stared in awe at the "many gray, hungry faces, all luminous like an El Greco painting; and all singing." Muggeridge listened as the compressed, reverent crowd lifted up hymns in praise of the ever-present Helper who alone could bring comfort, and he felt God near, near enough to touch. He was not just something spoken by the bearded priests up front, who chanted and swung their censers. He showed Himself specifically through one of the worshipers: "one of the gray faces, the grayest and most luminous of all."

When Norman Vincent Peale was a boy, he watched a man named Dave—the town drunk, wife beater, vile mouth, and all-around holy terror—come forward in his father's church after a strongly evangelistic sermon. Dave felt that God had come close to him, and he was moved. "I was awed by the look on his face," Peale wrote, "a look of wonder and inexpressible joy. It is printed on my memory to this day."

Most of the upstanding folk in Bowersville, Ohio, were sure Dave's "conversion" wouldn't last. They couldn't fathom a renegade changing in a minute. But Peale tells us that it in fact lasted a lifetime: "He became literally a saint, a new man in Christ, and for half a century he blessed the lives of everyone who knew him."

There's something to that "fulness of joy" celebrated in the psalms. It flashes forth when Someone big enough to take the starry hosts through their paces focuses His transcendent being into the confines of a human heart.

You open your hand

What the psalmists joyfully deposit in our hands and our hearts is a picture of the complete God. He does everything, and He does everything well. He's totally sovereign over all and yet completely the servant at our right hand. He's a consuming fire of justice and yet also a tender heart of mercy. He's eternal, unchanging, absolutely beyond, and yet a very personal face beaming right into ours. He is the complete God, and so we rejoice completely.

This is the God for everyone, in every situation. Whatever problems may entangle us, whatever dilemmas torture us, whatever weaknesses trip us up, He is there for us, here for us. However our genes and childhood and life traumas may have conspired to twist our psyche out of shape, He has the code to re-create us individually in His image.

> Both high and low among men
>   find refuge in the shadow of your wings.
> They feast on the abundance of your house;
>   you give them drink from your river of delights.
> For with you is the fountain of life;
>   in your light we see light.

In God's love we see love (sometimes for the first time); within God's wideness we are widened; under God's care we learn caring; in God's identity we find our own.

There's good reason to learn the language of joy; it opens up to our minds and hearts the complete God, the Rock of refuge, the Fortress who surrounds His people "as the mountains surround Jerusalem," the healer of the brokenhearted whose unfailing love and faithfulness extend to the heavens.

He is the Good Shepherd who takes us to green pastures and still waters, the One who "lifts the needy from the ash heap" and "seats them with princes," turns the barren woman into "a happy mother of children," "watches over the alien," "sustains the fatherless," and "upholds the cause of the oppressed."

The author of Psalm 145 sums it up with simple eloquence:

> You open your hand
>   and satisfy the desires of every living thing.

All these joyful exclamations in the psalms add up to one bottom line: a God who is capable of carrying us. Whatever our troubles, burdens, or bents, He can sustain the load.

In a letter to his wife, statesman and jurist Count Helmuth James von Moltke expressed amazement at the high spirits in which God had sustained him in January of 1945. He was about to be executed by the Nazis, yet he found himself pondering his last twenty-four hours, not in terror, but with a sense of blessedness.

Even at the trial, when the president of the "People's Court" roared at him and he knew there could be only one verdict, Moltke had felt secure. He wrote: "It was just as it is written in Isaiah 43:2—'When thou passest through the waters, I will be with thee; and through the rivers, they shall not overflow thee.'"

Moltke believed that God had been close, guiding him "firmly and clearly" during the last two days. "I am so full of thanks," the condemned man wrote, "that there is actually no room for anything else."

He felt grateful for the last visit with his wife, which assured him she was standing fast, and for the opportunity to put all his affairs in order. He realized that public censure had enabled him to let loose of all pride and rely more wholeheartedly on God's mercy and forgiveness. He'd been able to put the anguish of parting and fear of death behind him and now was "endowed with faith, hope, and love, all this in a plenitude truly lavish."

Because of all this, Moltke told his wife that "your husband stood before the Nazi judge not as a Protestant, not as a landed proprietor, not as a nobleman, not as a Prussian, not as a German—but as a Christian and nothing else."

Feeling greatly comforted, Moltke walked off to his execution.

On September 17, 1977, Joy Swift sat in a motel room trying to erase that terrible date, two days earlier, when she had arrived home to find ambulances and police cars surrounding her house and her four children murdered. The hours since then had been a blur of police interrogations, newspaper headlines, and searing pain.

Joy had to be alone. She sat on the floor facing the wall, closed her eyes, and plummeted into her feelings. "I felt like an empty fifty-five gallon drum, cold and hollow," Joy recalled. "The real me was a tiny speck inside the drum. This tiny speck was screaming for answers, but its words only echoed back in the cold, empty space."

This young, broken woman silently screamed for God to hear her. She told Him she couldn't live without the kids. They were her whole life. She begged Him to bring them back.

Her voice felt like an echo inside the steel drum. Then the echo faded. "A hole was punched in the side of the drum, and a fluid, warm and comforting, began to fill it," Joy said. "The tiny speck basked in the security of the fluid, like a fetus in its womb." For a long time she sat there relishing the peaceful calm.

Gradually, Joy was given the assurance that the kids were in God's hands. Then . . . "All of a sudden it felt as if all my children were sitting on my lap. My arms caressed the air around me as I imagined touching and holding them." And then in this tranquil quiet, Joy felt a voice telling her that she would be with them again.

Walking through the student union one day as an anonymous sophomore at Western Illinois University, I paused at a table loaded with books for two reasons: the smiling blonde behind it and the sign that read "InterVarsity Christian Fellowship." Trying not to ogle the InterVarsity representative too obviously, I scanned the titles and picked up *The God Who Is There*, by Francis Schaeffer. The girl recommended the book highly; I listened appreciatively and bought it. That proved to be the perfect ending to a great furlough.

A year earlier God had delivered me from a quirky obsession with doubt. I was able to stop compulsively defending the faith. But finding good reasons for it remained a concern. I'd always been interested in apologetics and the big questions. So for a while I kept in touch with the more respectable doubts.

Soon, however, I realized I needed more than freedom from an obsessive skepticism. I needed a clean break; I needed a vacation from apologetics. It was a burden that I wanted to let go for a while.

I asked the Lord for a year's furlough and got it with surprisingly little effort. God simply carried all the weighty philosophical problems for me. I lost touch.

Was this just a cop-out? Turn off brain, let God handle it? Not quite. At the end of that year or so, I walked by the table in the student union and discovered Francis Schaeffer. His book blew the lid off the defensive little box I had put Christian apologetics into. Here was the biblical world view competing and winning out in the world of art, philosophy, literature, and popular culture. I was swept off my feet. I had never dreamed Christianity provided such a thorough answer to all the big questions. God had carried me along to the perfect denouement.

The complete God carries all our burdens. He soothes anxious souls (like Helmuth von Moltke's), comforts broken hearts (like Joy Swift's), and eases troubled minds (like mine). A multitude who've fallen into His everlasting arms have found Him to be a humble, patient, giving Lord who sustains them.

Chapter 13
The Weapon of Praise

Everything that has breath

Antoine de Saint-Exupery, a French aviator flying the mails across the Sahara in the 1920s, was anxious to talk to the three Muslim chieftains returning from the trip of their lives. They'd been flown to France for a visit. Since the day of their birth, these nomads had seen only sand and desert scrub stretching from horizon to horizon. What would it be like for them to tour Paris, see the Eiffel Tower and Palace of Versailles?

Saint-Exupery asked. The tribesmen seemed rather indifferent. They granted that the Louvre was "very big." But technical progress had not impressed them. Locomotives, automobiles, telephones—they were curiosities, to be sure, but not curious enough to break the composure of Allah's proud warriors.

Then the three chieftains recalled a trip into the French Alps, and they could not speak for a moment. The memories moved them too deeply. Slowly Saint-Exupery coaxed the story out. A guide had led the three to a tremendous waterfall, a braided column of water that thundered over the rocks. The Sahara tribesmen tasted it. It was sweet.

Water! A thing worth its weight in gold. How many times had they marched for days to reach some well, where they had to dig deep for a few cupfuls of muddy liquid. When a little rain fell in the Sahara, tribes might ride 200 miles toward a bit of grass springing up in the sand.

The men stood transfixed. The guide tried to lead them away to the next scenic spot. They wouldn't budge: "Leave us here a little longer." The lifeblood of man was roaring out of the belly of a mountain. Here God was manifesting Himself, and they did not want to turn their backs.

"That's all there is to see," the guide said.

"We must wait," they insisted.

"Wait for what?"

"The end."

It was inconceivable that this torrent of liquid could just flow on and on. How could it never stop? The Sahara tribesmen were shaken to their roots. They wondered how Allah could possibly pour such unfathomable blessings on infidels.

Then the guide delivered a final blow: "But that water has been running for a thousand years!"

To really understand the 150 psalms of Scripture, we have to understand something of what those tribesmen from the Sahara felt. The psalmists are, in effect, staring at a waterfall rushing from the great Rock of Israel. He is above all, a wonder to be admired. His righteousness and lovingkindness just keep flowing on and on and on, inexhaustible. How does He keep having mercy on the people who keep turning their backs and stiffening their necks? Doesn't Yahweh ever get fed up?

It's difficult to fathom holiness going on and on. With heroic effort we manage to scratch out a few minutes of virtue in the self-centered rush of our days on earth—but here's Someone whose goodness never misses a beat.

His passion for justice rolls on, undiluted, uncompromising. He is a servant always there for us, the water of eternal life flowing on and on to be soaked up by many rags. His patience and compassion form an endless stream splashing around us.

Nothing in our morally barren world has prepared us for this sight. We stand transfixed before such an abundant Life; we gape at a Person eternally demonstrating His excellence. Nothing can make us budge.

That's what motivates the psalmists. They feel the same compulsion that drives the twenty-four elders of Revelation 4 to declare ceaselessly as they throw their crowns at the feet of the Almighty: "Holy, holy, holy . . ." Water, water, water, how does it keep flowing on?

The psalms come to a fitting climax in a rush of almost breathless praise that dominates the final songs in the book. Psalm 144 confidently lifts up the God of victory and prosperity. Psalm 145 pours out a flood of praise to the majesty and generosity of God the King. In Psalm 146 we find exalted the Lord who is our help in every need. Psalm 147 offers in its praises a vivid picture of the complete God who calls each star by name and provides for the young ravens when they call.

Then, in Psalms 148, 149, and 150, we come to the great invitations to praise that urge the reader to become participant. This is the point of the whole book: join in.

Psalm 148 tells us to get on the cosmic bandwagon. Sun, moon, and stars are doing it—by their inscrutable archs in the heavens. Rodents, birds, fruit trees, cattle, mountains, even sea creatures in the ocean depths—all know the tune. Creation in its fullness echoes with praise. So join with the stormy winds that do His bidding, join with the heavenly host, all you young men and maidens, old men and children, praise the God who thunders out His graces on and on like an inexhaustible waterfall.

Psalm 149 jumps right in with its refrains: Sing a new song, rejoice in your Maker, praise His name with dancing, sing for joy on your bed.

Finally, Psalm 150 provides us with a symphony of praise—the last crescendo of music from the heart, with cymbals clashing, to the God of surpassing greatness. Praise God with all your heart, with everything at your command, from your own shouts to the sound of trumpet, harp, lyre, strings, and flute. "Let everything that has breath praise the Lord."

No one can withstand you

What the psalmists are trying to communicate is that praise is good for us, an essential part of healthy life, not some esoteric practice reserved for mystics.

> How good it is to sing praises to our God,
> how pleasant and fitting to praise him!

As we've seen, the psalms have plenty of cries for help, cries of anguish, cries of vengeance. They are prayers from very human hearts. But the dominant message of the whole book is this: Praise is the most important component of our prayer life.

Of the 150 psalms, sixty-nine express nothing but praise and devotion. This is by far the largest category in the book. Many others, of course, mix praise with calls for help, confession, or moral teaching. Eleven psalms, for example, can be classified as appeals for justice. Six psalms focus in on the downfall of the writer's enemies. But sixty-nine are devoted to praise, and praise alone.

These psalmists saw praise, not as a religious accessory, but as a reason for living:

> It is not the dead who praise the Lord,
>   those who go down to silence;
> it is we who extol the Lord,
>   both now and forevermore.
> Praise the Lord.

When King Jehoshaphat heard that a vast allied army from Moab and Ammon was marching toward Jerusalem, he spread the matter before the Lord—and the people. His public prayer began: "'O Lord, God of our fathers, are you not the God who is in heaven? You rule over all the kingdoms of the nations. Power and might are in your hand, and no one can withstand you.'" In this hour of danger, Jehoshaphat remembered to praise.

Early the next morning the forces of Judah marched out to confront the invaders in the Desert of Tekoa, south of Jerusalem. Jehoshaphat decided to organize his troops in a very unusual way. At the very head of his army he placed a company of singers. These men dressed in holy attire and led the way with praises to God "for the splendor of his holiness."

As the men of Judah sang, God threw the invader's army into chaos. By the time Jehoshaphat's praising army arrived on the scene, the Desert of Tekoa was strewn with corpses.

Praise is a great weapon to be wielded. When the Assyrian king Sennacherib laid siege to Jerusalem, King Hezekiah presented the city's desperate straits to the Lord. The first words of Hezekiah's petition show where his gaze was firmly fixed: "'O Lord, God of Israel, enthroned between the cherubim, you alone are God over all

the kingdoms of the earth. You have made heaven and earth.'"
Hezekiah knew how to praise. And God responded to his faith. That
night 185,000 Assyrian soldiers died mysteriously. When
Sennacherib woke up, he saw a camp filled with dead bodies. The
besieger slipped back home to Nineveh.

Merlin Carothers has documented the power of praise quite
dramatically in his testimony *Prison to Praise*. In the book *Answers
to Praise* he tells story after story of people finding solutions to a
welter of problems—from simple discouragement to infidelity to
drug addiction. Carothers believes, and demonstrates, that God's
intervening power is unleashed when people adopt a pattern of
praise and thanksgiving in their lives. Most of us may not buy
praise power as the cure-all for every human difficulty, but it
certainly seems a greatly underrated resource.

The practice of praise is one of the greatest things we can do for
our emotional lives. Generally, negative emotions arise from our
thoughts getting co-opted by too many past petty irritants, distant
worries, or present failures. For some reason, we naturally adhere
to whatever is adverse around us and mull it over—and over. As the
Welsh proverb says, "Bad news goes about in clogs, good news in
stockinged feet." Perhaps all this is related to the gravity of our
sinful nature.

At any rate, focusing on the Person of God Himself is the best
way to cancel out the negatives. God is bigger than our problems,
better than our failures, more promising than our worries. He
simply outweighs everything—if we place Him in perspective.
Praise must be up close and personal, not just about God's acces-
sories, the blessings, what happens to us, but about Him, period.

God can be the great constant in our lives, a peaceful, still spot
for the here-and-thereness of our feelings. We may have blown it
badly, but there He is, as merciful as ever, the Rock of Ages,
looming over our difficulties. We may feel intimidated by a chronic
habit, but the Almighty crushes His adversaries in the dust. It's
been said that what we praise in other people is a sure indication
of our own character. But it's even more true that, in the Spirit,
praise to God creates character.

Praise means making an investment of emotion in the Person of
God. Too many of us are connected to Him only by a few stilted

thoughts sent His way. We wave at Him in the distance. Our mental activity heats up in all kinds of situations and for all kinds of causes—except the Lord of heaven and earth. We've got to invest of ourselves in the language of praise. When we do, we will find that it can sustain us during the worst of times.

Merrill Womach's small private plane didn't clear the trees at the end of the runway on Thanksgiving Day, 1961. It whipped around and plunged through icy branches to the ground. When Womach, gospel singer and businessman, regained consciousness, he saw flames all around him. Before he could scramble out, his legs, arms, chest, and head were badly burned.

Womach couldn't see, but he stumbled through the deep snow toward the sounds of a nearby highway.

Fortunately, two men saw the plane go down and rushed to the scene in a station wagon. Womach looked like a monster with no eyes, nose, mouth, his head was charred and swollen.

The men placed him gently in the back of the car and drove off toward a hospital. He lay there feeling the terrible pain sweep over him. But, as Womach recalled, "an incredible thing happened . . . I felt like singing."

Forcing one eye open, he looked down at his ghastly hand and began to realize how badly he'd been burned. But as they moved down Highway 97, Womach's feeling persisted: "My head was swelling and the pain grew more and more intense," he said. "Still I felt like singing. It was an old gospel song I had learned as a child. I don't know why that song came rushing out of me instead of cries of pain and pity, but it did."

As the two men in the front seat listened in disbelieving silence, these words emerged from a crack in Womach's blackened face:

> I've found the dear Savior and now I'm made whole;
> I'm pardoned and have my release.
> His Spirit abiding and blessing my soul,
> Praise God, in my heart there is peace.

At Collier State Park an ambulance met the station wagon. The attendants transferred Merrill on a stretcher and raced away. Through the scream of the siren and through Womach's own loud pain, the song still emerged unchanged, lyrics intact, a tune with eternal resonance:

> Wonderful peace, Wonderful peace,
> Peace that the world cannot give.
> When I think how He brought me
> From darkness to light,
> There's a wonderful, wonderful peace.

My heart is steadfast

All the languages of the heart that are expressed in the psalms—the expressions of despair and hope, of pleading and wonder, of joy and remembering—flow into this most powerful of idioms: praise. It's the most therapeutic language of the heart known to man.

But the psalmists don't pretend that one learns this speech automatically. We are, of course, much more inclined to cry for help than exult in praise. What the psalmists demonstrate is a determination to practice this spiritual discipline, period. They've got to have it in their lives.

These poets know the value of persistence:

> My heart is steadfast, O God;
> I will sing and make music with all my soul.

They determine to do it wholeheartedly:

> I will extol the Lord with all my heart
> in the council of the upright and in the assembly.

They make it a consistent, daily habit:

> It is good to praise the Lord
> and make music to your name, O Most High,
> to proclaim your love in the morning
> and your faithfulness at night.

They determine never to give up on this essential language:

> I will sing to the Lord all my life;
> I will sing praise to my God as long as I live.

So how do we get started? First, we've got to think about God as a Person with certain qualities, not just as a Being who gives us things. We find it pretty easy to thank Him for nice days, good grades, and new cars; we can click off our blessings. But praise is about God Himself—looking into the face of the loved One, not just thinking about what we can get out of Him.

Mark Twain's wife detested her famous husband's habit of swearing and tried many times to reform the man's tongue. One day the writer cut himself while shaving and blew through his entire store of expletives. When he'd finished, his wife steadily repeated every phrase. Twain turned from the mirror and replied, "You have the words, dear, but you don't know the tune."

Often in our praise (which is the counterpart of cursing) we recite the words without really getting the tune. Something must jog us into praise; we need the moral equivalent of hammering our thumb. That's the stimulus that will help us praise with something equivalent to the gusto of a sailor spewing epithets. Here are some suggestions on how to start growing in the skill of praise.

Paraphrase a psalm. The psalms contain a rich variety of praises to God. To get your own habit of praise started, try paraphrasing a psalm that you like. Repeat its expressions of admiration to God in your own words. Make it your own prayer. The devotion and awe of the psalms are contagious. Looking through them toward God will stimulate you toward creative praise of your own.

Make a praise collection. In the psalms and in other portions of Scripture, there are usually verses of praise describing the character and glory of God that we find particularly striking. Begin to write down those favorite descriptions. Make your own collection of praise that fills out the character of God in living color.

As you collect these examples of praise, you will find your picture of God continues to expand. The richness of God's character will grow more vivid in your mind. You will discover that the God whose voice shakes the earth and whose presence causes mountains to melt like wax is also the God who gently promises not to break a bruised reed or snuff out a dimly burning wick. You discover that the God who stills the tumult of the peoples is also the God who causes the dawn and sunset to shout for joy.

Focus on one character trait. As you become experienced in praise you will want, during some prayers, to look closely at specific aspects of God's person and character. This helps to sharpen your concentration and deepen your insight. Select something like power, holiness, or mercy, and think of all the biblical descriptions you can recall that relate to one quality. Think of God's acts in Scripture that exemplify that quality. Now you can praise God for the ways He is powerful, holy, merciful, etc.

It is even more effective when we can remember acts of God we ourselves have witnessed that exemplify the trait we are concentrating on. Thinking of God's aid and blessing in our lives intensifies our adoration.

Praise is the language that looks directly at the Lord of the universe. The glimpses it gives us can enlarge our lives immeasurably. I'll never forget the time that praise burst into my rather confined, sheltered life.

The churches in which I grew up were removed some distance from the exuberance of the psalms. We worshiped a quiet God on quiet Sabbaths in quiet small towns. Only tidy, unobtrusive miracles were acknowledged from the pulpit.

God was almighty in theory. But the celebration of religion around me did not reflect that. The whining organ and frail voices of the elderly did not inspire my young ears. I felt an obligation to witness. It hung over my head ominously. Yet I found it hard to speak to that huge, alien world out there from our isolated subculture. I believed sincerely, but in a corner. I never saw my faith echoed widely and was self-conscious about my "peculiar" beliefs. Then, I went to Dallas.

Eighty thousand high-school and college kids filled the Cotton Bowl to the brim and buzzed with an excitement I shared. Campus Crusade's Explo '72 was turning us on to "sharing Jesus." We'd grown bold in the city that week; the world seemed to be opening up to faith. Now I looked out at a stadium filled with restive Jesus people. "Give me a J," a youthful announcer called. Eighty thousand voices roared back a "J!" that shook the vast circle of seats. This beat the whining organ all to pieces. I yelled with newfound gusto as Jesus cheers echoed back and forth from one bank of the stadium to the other.

Rain came one day and threatened to dampen the evening meeting. But no one wanted to leave. The songs went on as we huddled in the drizzle. Then the clouds bunched together and darkened; suddenly, thunder roared across the sky above us. In an instant we were on our feet roaring back. Thunder echoed again. Again we cheered lustily. Happy now to be in the elements, we carried on our boisterous dialogue for five minutes. Then the drizzle slackened, the lightning ceased, speakers came to the stage, and we settled down to listen to lesser voices.

Explo '72 broke all my inhibitions. God had busted out into the open. He no longer occupied a little corner of life. He thundered out over the whole world—and I could cheer back.

That stadium full of praise turned me from spectator into participant in the joyful worship of Psalms. But one almost unnoticed incident showed me the real power of that language.

I was walking toward my seat in the stadium through one of the upper-level entryways when I spotted an elderly couple standing there, pressed against the concrete wall, their faces lifted up, enraptured.

In one brief moment as I passed, they painted an unforgettable portrait in my mind. The couple clung together and whispered, their joy electric between them. I wondered why they didn't go in and take a seat. Then I noticed both were blind. Unwilling to occupy a place in the crowded stadium a sighted person might want, they stood where they could hear those praises echoing big and bold. And they seemed to bless, without a word, every person that brushed past.

I have never seen faces say more. They were bright and tender, not at all the blank stares one might expect. Their rejoicing seemed so different from the easy happiness of the rest of us, jumping up toward heaven with youthful energy. Their praise had been carved out of isolation, but they were there exulting with us, transcending the dark.

Sources

Unless otherwise identified, all texts are from the book of Psalms and the New International Version.

Chapter One

(page)	(reference)	(source)
5	no struggles	Psalm 73:4, 5
8	forsaken me	22:1
8	stand far off	10:1
8	Shout louder	1 Kings 18:27
9	Awake, O Lord!	Psalm 44:23, 24
9	rejected us	74:2
9	hold back	74:11
9	against prayers	80:4
9	broken down	80:12
11	beast before you	73:22, 23
11	Whom have I	73:25

Chapter Two

17	depths, grave	30:1, 3
17	out of deep waters	18:16
17	awesome deeds	65:5
18	place of abundance	66:12
18	stouthearted	138:3
18	setting me free	118:5, 6

Chapter Three

23	Mr. Thompson	Oliver Sacks, *The Man Who Mistook His Wife for a Hat* (New York: Harper & Row, 1985), pp. 108-112.
24	God was Rock	78:35
24	not forget	78:7
27	Many O Lord	40:5
27	I remember	143:5, 6
27	but flesh	78:39
27, 28	meditate on	77:12
28	remember wonders	105:5

Chapter Four

34	my confidence	71:5
34	Ethan	89:50, 1, 2
34	downcast	42:5
34	watchmen	130:6
34	weaned child	131:2, 3
35	new birth	1 Peter 1:3
36	forgotten	31:11, 12
36	utterly crushed	38:8, 13, 17
36	up to my neck	69:1, 2
37	worn out	6:6, 7
37	promises peace	85:8-12
39	oppressed me	129:2, 3
39	no one is concerned	142:4
39	I was silent	39:2, 3